C000049930

Co

To Stuart, my companion in life and on the road

The Author (and her husband)

Stuart and I met at Glasgow University in 1961. For me it was the third life-changing event of that year. I had just been in Germany where I had worked as a volunteer among post-war displaced persons and stayed in a refugee camp with a Polish woman whom I'd been writing to since school days. The Berlin Wall closed the day before I left Germany, a truly apocalyptic moment, as was my fifty-five year old mother's diagnosis of Parkinson's Disease, which overshadowed my and my sister's lives for the next nineteen years.

Stuart meantime had just returned from his first visit to the USSR and his second visit to Poland. I said, "Tell me all about Poland." He said, "Would you like to learn Polish?" And the consequence . . . we're still at it!

Stuart taught Russian in York University, then became an Anglican priest. We started visiting Christian dissidents in Moscow and Leningrad in 1984, lived in St Petersburg between 1991 and 1998, and then Poland. The surviving fragment of the Warsaw Ghetto wall was in our courtyard which led me to research Jewish Warsaw, I had already published *Ghetto* (Lion Publishing 1989) and then *Don't go Uncle's Wedding* (Azure/SPCK 2000) I also began to research the life and work of a Polish author, Zofia Nałkowska which led to a biography *From Corsets to Communism* (Scotland Street Press 2019).

Other books by Jenny Robertson:
The Fortune Teller of Philippi (Bridge House Publications)
Wojtek, War Hero Bear (Birlinn Publishing)
From the Volga to the Clyde (http://www.flemingpublications.com)

UKRAINE

a personal exploration
before Putin's invasion

Jenny Robertson

British Library Cataloguing in Publication Data:
a catalogue record for this publication
is available from the British Library

ISBN   978-1-912052-81-3

Typeset in 12pt Minion Pro at Haddington, Scotland

Printing and cover design by
West Port Print and Design, St Andrews

Acknowledgments

Writing a book is a solo activity but bringing it to publication requires team work. So thank you Jock Stein and Handsel Press for making time in a busy agenda to produce this personal exploration of western Ukraine.

Thank you Elizabeth Sadler for your work on the map. You've wonderfully put together the jigsaw-like pieces of imagery I sent you. A big thank you to David Healey for your help with the photographs. You advised me about dimensions and colour and helped me find the best links for downloads. Thank you, Krystyna Szumelukowa for introducing me to your dear friend Joseph Tarnowski and setting me on the road to Lutsk.

Thanks go to Dr Maria Chamberlain for permission to quote the extract from her mother's letter on page 28.

Thank you Matthew Zajac for taking time to read a pre-proof copy of the book and for your kind commendation . . . and also thanks to Martin Stepek for use of his earlier one.

I want to thank my sister Margaret for patiently reading an early draft of the book. You've been my writing mentor since our early teens, my first editor, keenest critic and often my only reader. Your comments helped me find a sharper focus.

And thank you my dear readers. After a lifetime of writing this is very likely my last ever publication, which makes me so grateful to Jock and to all of you for your interest and support.

A big thank you to: https://ukraine.ua/imagebank/ for stunning pictures. This book isn't a commercial proposition, and we are so aware of the devastation suffered by whole cities and most of all by people in Ukraine. Your purchase of this book will support the provision of books for Ukrainian refugee children in Edinburgh.

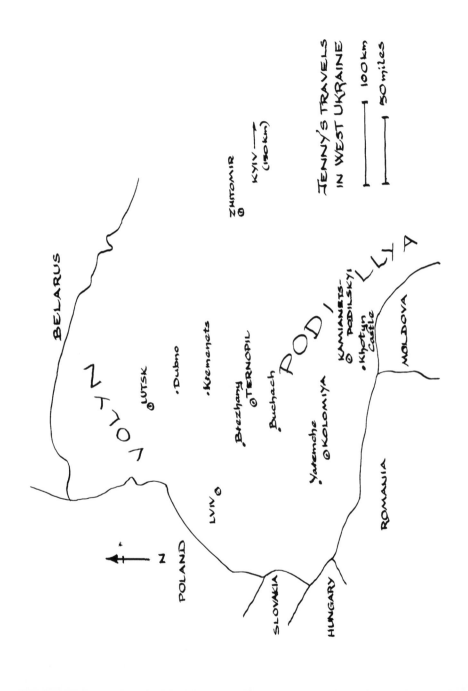

JENNY'S TRAVELS IN WEST UKRAINE

├─┤ 100 km
├─┤ 50 miles

BELARUS

POLAND

SLOVAKIA

HUNGARY

ROMANIA

MOLDOVA

VOLYN

PODILLYA

ZHITOMIR ⊕

KYIV ⟶ (150km)

⊕ LUTSK

. Dubno

. Kremenets

Brezhany ⊕ TERNOPIL

. Buchach

Yaremche . ⊕ KOLOMIYA

LVIV ⊕

KAMIANETS- ⊕ PODILSKYI

. Khotyn Castle

N

vi

Chapter 1

Kyiv

Ukraine is the second largest country on the European continent, where west meets east, where the south meets the Black Sea and once met the Ottoman Empire. The very name tells us that we're on the edge of things: *U* means at, like *chez* in French while *kraj* translates as edge or border.

The language is East Slavonic, it's written in Cyrillic, a form of writing promoted by two brothers, Cyril and Methodius over a thousand years ago to accommodate the phonetics of Slavonic. Because of the close kinship of the Slav countries many customs are common to them all. You should never shake hands across the threshold. You should never offer an odd number of flowers to your hostess and you should always sit down for a minute before you embark on a journey. Foreigners, unfamiliar with this custom, check their phones and rush for the taxi, but it's actually helpful, after the mad rush of packing, to sit and be still – the chances are you'll remember something essential that's been forgotten.

Ukrainian, Polish and Czech use Slavonic names for the months of the year, mostly connected with nature. They all love beetroot soup but they make it in different ways.

I knew about Ukraine indirectly from my studies in Polish and Russian. I even shared a room in Warsaw with a Ukrainian academic. That was in the days of the politburo's iron grip and she never identified herself as Ukrainian, just as a Soviet citizen. So Ukraine, that country on the edge, stayed on the edge of my horizon until 2005 when we receive news that puts a big smile on my husband Stuart's face. He's been asked to be locum chaplain to the Anglican congregation in Kyiv.

I don't want to go. We have just lived seven years in St Petersburg, minus a year when I was back in Edinburgh and went through treatment for breast cancer. We then spent six years in Poland where Stuart, a Scottish Episcopal priest, served in the Anglican chaplaincy in Warsaw and then a year in Barcelona. It's time we put our roots down at home. Not a bit. "To Rus', to Rus'," my husband declares, like the Polish hussars of old. "You don't even need a visa if you only stay ninety days."

Oh great! I can just see him mounting his milk white steed and riding off into the sunrise courtesy of KLM.

"I'll come for one month," I compromise. "And only if we travel and see something of Ukraine."

This book is my personal encounter with people and their stories, visits to castles, churches and deserted synagogues as well as to busy markets, eating places, forest walks and train travel. We shall hear about lost kingdoms and Cossacks, freedom fighters and bears – and mushrooms. All from journeys between 2005 and 2018.

Scythians, Sarmatians, Slavs and Scandinavians, plus 'gentle' Saint Andrew

The story of the extensive land of Ukraine goes back to pre-history. It comes into written history with the Greeks and especially with the genial historian Herodotus (c. 484 – c. 425 BC) who writes about the fertility of the land around the Black Sea coasts and about its inhabitants, the Scythians, nomadic warriors, famed for their horsemanship. They could shoot arrows backwards (as depicted on stones from ancient Assyria), spoke broken Greek and were famously brutal. They scalped their victims, used the hairy tops as napkins and drank from the skull. Scythian women were feared warriors and ace archers who supposedly cut off their right breast (ouch!) to accommodate their bows.

St Paul's epistle to the church in Colossae (see 3:11) distinguishes the Scythians from other barbarians: there is no longer Greek and Jew, circumcised and uncircumcised, barbarian, Scythian, slave and free . . .

The Scythians left fabulous golden objects in burial mounds across Ukraine. Many of these grave goods were later taken to Russia and can be seen in the Hermitage Museum in St Petersburg. Archaeology confirms Herodotus' writings. Excavations have uncovered warriors buried with their horses, one grave had fifteen horses along with grave goods and slaves. One warrior princess was buried with a murdered male who, it is thought, had been killed to protect her on her journey to the afterlife.

In time the Scythians were displaced by another tribe, the Sarmatians. In fact we can give a quick overview of Ukraine's origins with the letter S: Scythians, Sarmatians, Scandinavians and Slavs.

The Sarmatians, like the Picts in Scotland have faded from history, but left their mark on later Polish-Ruthenian (Ukrainian) aristocracy who liked to wear a splendid Turkish-style caftan and wrap an elaborately embroidered scarf around a capacious stomach well filled with bear steaks, wild boar and venison caught in the hunt. This was considered a Sarmatian lifestyle.

The Slavs come onstage around the sixth century AD. They are recorded by early historians as being widely dispersed over Ukraine, the Balkans and Poland, either as forest dwellers or as agriculturalists, in fact the name Poland comes from the word for field.

A Byzantine historian, Procopius, states disdainfully that the Slavic tribes lived "in pitiful hovels . . . at all times covered with filth . . ." But, importantly, they 'are not ruled by one man, but they have lived from old under a democracy, and consequently everything that involves their welfare, whether for good or ill, is referred to the people.'[1]

In the eleventh century, a monk-historian in Kyiv who wrote the important *Primary Chronicle*, notes that St Andrew visited the lands around the Black Sea and wandered beside the River Dnipro. Thus the Ukrainian churches claim their origins from 'Andrew, the first called' as he is referred to in the Eastern Orthodox liturgy.

Here we have a link with Scotland, for a monk named Regulus or Rule took Andrew's bones to the east coast town which bears the saint's name.

St Andrew was more complimentary about the personal hygiene of the Slavs than the historian Procopius had been. The saint recounted how the Slavs build a wooden bath house which they fill with steam, so hot you could hardly bear it, lash themselves with branches and then pour cold water over themselves.

---

1   Serhii Plokhy, *The Gates of Europe*, Penguin, Random House UK 2015, 15,16.

They do indeed. In Russia it's called a *banya* and it's one of the best cures from the stresses of the long Russian winter.

The ancient Scythians filled the steam with marijuana and got high as well as clean.

One more word from St Andrew. The story goes that as he walked by the River Dnipro he looked up at the hills (a true Scotsman!) and prophesied that a great city with many churches would be built upon those hills. As a sign that this would come to pass, the saint planted his cross on the hill top, and Kyiv was eventually founded there.

So here are the Slavs, some in the fields, some in the forests, either living in squalor (Procopius) or keeping quite strenuously clean (St Andrew). Various tribes come and go, including people called the Khazars who built up important trading links along the Silk Road.

But now, wait for it, here come the heavy mob. The Scandinavians or Vikings.

These tribes set off in their longboats along the rivers of Ukraine. Their aim was trade, but a bit of pillage and plunder on the way wouldn't go wrong, although the forest lands of the Slavs didn't offer too much in the way of plunder, except for slaves to cut down trees for rollers and drag those long boats overland.

Their first settlement Staraya (old) Ladoga, is in Russia on the River Volkhov, where there have been recent attempts to reconstruct the Viking past, claimed now as the foundation of Russia itself. I visited it once and savoured delicious potato pancakes, *draniki* – a recipe from Belarus, but a favourite all over the Slavonic world.

Old Ladoga has links with Scotland and our own Queen Margaret because two Saxon princes sought asylum there. One of them, Edward Atheling (the Prince) later became the father of Margaret, Queen of Scotland.

Having founded Ladoga, the Swedish Vikings (with Norwegians and Finns among them) pushed south through forests and down rivers where a Viking called Rurik established the city of Novgorod (new town) now in Russia.

The Scandinavian forces had designs on Byzantium. They tussled with the Khazars on the way and won the city we now call Kyiv. This was the beginning of Rus', the name that Ukraine was first known by. One story says it's because the Vikings were red-headed. Others that it derives from the Finnish name for the Swedes, *Ruotsi* or else from the word to row (as in rowing boat, not quarrel). Russia also shares these origins, but it would emerge as a power to be reckoned with only in the eleventh century as Muscovy.

And now, with huge simplification of dates, battles and pillage, here we are at last in Kyivan Rus'; this name was given by later historians, while the people we know as Ukrainians were called Ruthenians, or Rusyns, a name that persisted until the twentieth century.

The founding of Kyiv

There's a legend that three brothers, Kyi, Shchek and Koryv set off in a longboat, guided by their sister Lybid who directed her brothers to three hills (the ones St Andrew had blessed). They built settlements there while Lybid gave her name to a nearby lake.

Archaeological evidence shows that there was indeed a fortified settlement on the hilltop in the sixth century.

Let's decide how to pronounce the name of city we used to call Kiev. TV newscasters call it *Keev*. Wrong. They've missed out the first syllable. Think *kick*. That's right, get that *i* sound right. Not *ee*, but a good short *i*, followed by *ee*. So K *y* (as in *kick*) *eev* will get closer to the Ukrainian way of saying the name of the capital.

Settled by Scandinavian/Slavic princes, the rulers gradually converted to Christianity.

First came Queen Olha. This formidable woman had put not a few people to death before her baptism in 955 when she was over sixty. She's now the patron saint of Kyiv. The story of her baptism has a nice twist, she received the blessings of Byzantine Christianity and also managed to outwit the Byzantine Emperor himself, who said that now she was a Christian, he wanted to marry her. After the baptism the Emperor summoned her and said, "I desire myself to wed thee." She replied, "How canst thou desire to wed me, when thou thyself didst christen me and call me 'daughter': thou well knowest how that is not lawful to

Christians." And the Emperor said, "O, Olga, thou hast outwitted me."[2] (Olha is the Ukrainian for the Russian name Olga.)

Christianity didn't take root, Olha's sons returned to paganism until her grandson, Prince Volodymyr brings the Viking story to an end.

According to the *Primary Chronicle* the pagan Prince Volodymyr sent ambassadors to learn about the four main religions, Judaism, Islam and the two forms of Christianity, western and eastern.

The ambassadors brought back reports that Judaism was a righteous religion based on holy law, but pork was forbidden, though wine was permitted. Islam forbade both the eating of pork and the drinking of alcohol – a turn-off for Volodymyr. However Islam – and this undoubtedly interested Volodymyr, permitted polygamy. Volodymyr was "insatiable in fornication . . . a lover of women, like Solomon." But he still had to hear about Christianity. He sent ambasadors westwards who brought back reports of a Pope who reigned supreme as a temporal as well as a spiritual ruler, which didn't suit Volodymyr. They also added, "We saw no beauty in their churches." However the ambassadors who went to Byzantium came back with glowing reports. They had seen the marvellous church of St Sophia in Constantinople and declared that they were at a loss for words:

> We knew not whether we were in heaven on earth. For on earth there is no such splendour or such beauty and we are at a loss how to describe it. We only know that God dwells there among men and their service surpasses the ceremonies of other nations. We cannot forget that beauty . . .[3]

And if that were not enough, an extra nudge was given: "Your grandmother Olha who was the wisest of all people also chose the Greek system . . ."

So Volodymyr embraced Christianity in its Eastern Orthodox form in 988, toppled the statue of the Slav god of thunder and led his country

---

2 *Old Russian Chronicles*, quoted Jenny Robertson, *Windows to Eternity*, BRF Oxford 1999, 58-59.
3 Ibid.

in baptism. An important turning point had been reached which impacted on all the later story of Ukraine and indeed of Europe.

It's noteworthy that Russia too traces its Christian beginnings to 988 under the ruler they call Vladimir. *Vlad* means ruler and *mir* means, confusingly, both peace and world. So Vladimir is either the ruler of the world or the ruler of peace. We can take our pick.

The exiled Saxon prince Edward Atheling and his brother Edmund left Ladoga and received a warm welcome at the court of Volodymyr's son Prince Yaroslav the Wise. Prince Edward and his brother then moved to Hungary where the girl who was to become Queen Margaret of Scotland, wife of King Malcolm Canmore was born.

Yaroslav ruled Rus from 1019 to his death in 1054. He encouraged literacy and law. He built the great Golden Gate of Kyiv as well as the impressive Cathedral of St Sophia, the Holy Wisdom, thus making his city as glorious as Byzantium. Rus' had entered a golden age.

Two hundred years later dark clouds loomed on the eastern horizon. In 1240 the grandson of Genghis Khan conquered Kyiv while the Grand Duchy of Lithuania took over the north west. Centres of culture and tolerance too often become easy prey for self-interested powers. The kingdom was torn apart by petty princes, later colonised by Lithuanian and Polish nobility, invaded, divided, struggled for freedom and finally was absorbed into the USSR.

So much for the beginnings, now a big jump forward to a new millennium which is when I begin my part of the story.

It's the end of September. Stuart has been in Kyiv for a month and I've just joined him. We're sitting outdoors in a café in town. Large yellowing leaves drift from trees that line the pavement.

The trees aren't the only things that line the pavement. Cars are parked the length of the road, expensive limousines with darkened windows, the mark of the corrupt business world that has flourished in formerly Communist Kyiv.

As we drink our coffee I tell Stuart about my change-over in Amsterdam. The departure lounge was full of Orthodox Jewish men in traditional black coats, large hats and side locks. One blew a *shofar*, the horn that is used at Rosh Hashanah, Jewish New Year. It turned out that they were on pilgrimage to Uman in central Ukraine, to pray at the *ohel* or tomb of a well-beloved Hasidic master, Rabbi Nachman of Bratslav. I couldn't help wondering how this influx of Orthodox Jewish men in their distinctive dress would be received in Ukraine with long memories of the Holocaust. I read later that although the annual pilgrimage to Rabbi Nachman's grave is welcome for the money the tourists bring to the town, it does indeed stir up negative if not anti-Semitic responses.

But now, here I am in Kyiv, not before time, says Stuart; he has quite a lot to show me.

Please remember that I am using my experiences before Putin's full-scale invasion in February 2022.

The Golden Gates and the Monastery of the Caves

We begin our tour at the site of the Golden Gates built by Yaroslav the Wise to emulate the splendid gates of Constantinople. Destroyed first by the Mongol invaders, rebuilt in wood and destroyed many more times, these present gates were put up by the Soviet regime when Ukraine was controlled from the Kremlin. The Soviet version is rather splendid, but doesn't seem quite genuine.

Our next stop is Yaroslav's Cathedral, St Sophia with its golden domes, its vast precincts, great domed ceiling, historic icons and frescoes; the best and most moving date back to the 11th century. Amazingly this great church survived the Second World War, although its neighbour the church and monastery of St Michael, now splendidly rebuilt, did not. The cathedral even survived the ravages of Stalinism because it was turned into a museum, which it still is. It's a huge mercy that St Sophia, once the beating heart of Yaroslav's city, has been preserved, but it has lost its soul. There's no smell of candles or incense, no devout old ladies bowing and crossing themselves, no young people either, no prayer at all.

It's to be hoped that the Cathedral, a UNESCO World Heritage site, will in future become a place of worship and prayer once again.

The other important UNESCO World Heritage site is most definitely a place of prayer and also of pilgrimage.

When Volodymyr accepted Christianity in 988, a monk called Anthony created a cave retreat in the city we know as the Ukrainian capital where he established an underground monastery. Here monks shut themselves away from daylight and starlight to pray and meditate. Here the first great histories of Rus' were written, art was made and Kyiv became a major cultural centre. Eight beautiful cathedral churches and a huge bell tower were built above ground, only to succumb to the vicissitudes of war and be rebuilt time and time again. The gorgeous golden domes shine above the river and dwarf the huge metal female figure of the Motherland. The Pechersk Lavra or Cave Monastery is a defining icon of Kyiv, a centre of pilgrimage from all over Ukraine, a loud, triumphant shout like a Bach *Hosanna*.

USPENSKY CATHEDRAL, PECHERSK LAVRA [*PHOTO BY STAS BURYAK*]

Once the eight churches had been built, the caves became a burial place where, miraculously, the monks' bodies haven't decayed. They're now a focus of pilgrimage and, in 2023 a place of contention as the whole monastery complex is controlled by the Moscow (as opposed to Ukrainian) Patriarchate. The clergy and their leadership are suspected of being actively in support of Putin's invasion.

We visit the Caves with a devoutly Orthodox friend. I have major difficulties with caves. I just don't like them. Even Fingal's Cave in Staffa is too much for me. I never venture in, just stand at the edge and listen to the churning waves. Much as I appreciate Eastern Orthodoxy, I find it hard to embrace a spirituality which seeks darkness underground. I prefer those Celtic monks who made their hermitages on cliff tops or copied out the Scriptures "while blackbirds sing above my well-ruled book . . . happily I write beneath the trees".[4]

As we emerge from the darkness I see that my friend's face is transformed by what has been for her, and is for so many, a deeply spiritual experience.

Sightseeing is tiring. We need to shop and eat, find places to relax. We find a shop with our favourite Borodinsky bread, a tasty dark rye loaf flavoured with caraway and coriander and thick dark syrup. The lady who serves us is delighted that we love her bread.

During our time in Kyiv we shop in small local supermarkets or in a large covered market. I love markets. I'm a glutton for fresh, home grown food, honey from the hive, mushrooms from the forest and chickens happily innocent of battery farming, freshly caught and plucked. Did I say fresh? Oh dear, disappointment! That organic hen turns out to be as tough as the proverbial old shoe leather.

There are many nice places to eat in Kyiv. We like a place close to our flat where the food is home cooked, inexpensive and popular for family groups but, like so many other eateries, it's beyond the reach of some local people we know through the Anglican congregation in Kyiv. This community meets in St Catherine's German Lutheran church on, guess what, Lutheran Street. The nineteenth century building is up a steep

---

4   Irish ninth century, displayed beside the Book of Kells in Trinity College, Dublin.

hill; all Kyiv is either uphill or downhill (like Edinburgh). We have to thank Lybid and St Andrew for a great location close to the river and high on a hill – and also thank the funicular which carries us up to enjoy views over the golden domes and yellowing leaves of hundreds of trees. Lutheran Street is close to the Presidential Palace where the vista is viewed by armed guards. We don't know in 2005 that the president will be another Volodymyr, this time Zelenskiy.

There's so much to see in Kyiv, I'll mention some favourite places.

Andryiyvskiy uzviz

St Andrew gave his name to this steep street, a nightmare in winter when the cobbles are like a skating rink. I'm a sucker for open air stalls even if they sell kitsch, as heaps of them do, but many are genuine and on the street too are galleries of folk art, and buskers and artists.

At the top of the street is the home of a Soviet writer, Mikhail Bulgakov. It's a museum now and I've heard rumours (in 2023) that it may be closed down because Bulgakov was ethnically Russian. He suffered repression and censorship under the Soviets, although Stalin favoured one of his plays. His best known books are *The White Guard* (1925) and the epic novel, *The Master and Margarita*, a critique of the Soviet system that couldn't be published until 1966, long after Bulgakov's death.

There are many art galleries in Kyiv; one which Stuart and I find quite amazing is a private museum in a splendid house that belonged to a wealthy business man and his wife, Bohdan and Varvara Khanenko in the nineteenth century. It's crammed with Old Masters and artefacts from all over the world – Bohdan and Varvara were knowledgeable collectors.

One small room contains an icon so rare that it can be considered unique. This Madonna and Child predates the destruction of icons in the eight century when a Roman Emperor, Leo III decreed that all religious art should be destroyed. It's a great loss that so much very early Christian art was wiped out for ever. Only about fifty-three early works survive including the Kyiv Madonna displayed in this museum, not hanging with the Old Masters, but in a separate small room, along with a very early icon of John the Baptist, another of two martyrs and two other saints.

These works of art have been beautifully and knowledgeably described by the art historian, Sister Wendy Beckett, who at the age of seventy seven set out on a quest to find this icon in Kyiv. The ladies at the cash desk at the Khanenko museum tell us about the arrival of this frail visitor. Her nun's habit was soaked after a snowstorm. She mounted the long and challenging staircase – and burst into tears when she saw the icon she had come so far to find.

"She just broke down in tears, and sobbed and sobbed," the ladies tell us. "We brought her a chair and she stayed in front of the icon for a long time."

We admire it too, a depiction so different from later icons that an Orthodox friend who saw a copy couldn't believe it was a true icon. There's more emotion in this early work and perhaps a deeper insight into a real human being, rather than a stylised figure who points to heaven away from our suffering world.

Sister Wendy writes of the icon, "Mary is urgent with the need, not to protect us, but to protect Jesus from us, to show us our own inner destructiveness."[5]

Given the destruction that lay ahead for Ukraine in 2022, Sister Wendy's interpretation of the icon is truly profound. And that terrible inner destructiveness that murders innocent people is starkly manifest in a place of massacre, Babyn Yar, as it is known in Ukrainian. Stuart and I visit this killing field.

They were told to bring warm clothes

On 21st June 1941 Hitler broke his pact with Stalin and invaded Eastern Europe. The Germans entered Kyiv on 19th September 1941. Ten days later, on the eve of the sacred fast, Yom Kippur, a great crowd of Jewish citizens left Kyiv for an unspecified – but surely safer – destination. They took with them the permitted number of possessions, including warm clothing. So convincing were the lies written up on posters in German, Ukrainian and Russian that people readily obeyed the Nazi orders to pack up and go. They realised the terrible truth when

5   *Encounter with God, in quest of the ancient icons of Mary*, London 2009, 100.

it was too late. Surrounded by barbed wire and machine gun fire, young people, parents, grandparents, tots and toddlers, were forced to give up their possessions, strip off their clothes and lie face downwards in deep pits to be shot and trampled down to make room, dead or still alive, for the next layer of victims.

Babyn Yar was a killing place all through the German occupation: Roma people, including children, Ukrainian freedom fighters, psychiatric patients, 'undesirables' of all sorts were murdered there and their bodies were buried in the soft sandy soil.

No words express this horror.

Long ago I noted these words by the Jewish philosopher Martin Buber (1878 – 1965):

> When you want to heave a person out of sludge and ordure (*Schlamm und Kot*), don't imagine that you can stay up above and feel good at reaching out a helping hand. You must go right down into the sludge and ordure, clasp the person with a strong hand and bring them and yourself up to the light. [*my translation*]

Nobody reached down into the hell that was Babyn Yar. Soldiers of the Wehrmacht were responsible for the appalling slaughter and so were their auxiliaries. These men included Ukrainians, who had already tasted Stalinist terror and state-induced famine in which millions died; they thought that Hitler might be a better deal to oust Stalin and help them bring about a free Ukraine. Instead they were co-opted into genocide. Local people too watched the Jews of Kyiv, their friends and neighbours walk to their deaths, yet no-one spoke out and four months later the infamous Wannsee conference shockingly rubber stamped the total extermination of all the Jews of Europe.

We look and walk, we pause and wonder. Yellow leaves float from the trees that shroud this vast terrain. I gather some in memory of murdered people.

A castle on a rock

We board a night train, settle into our bunks between starched sheets and head for a historic town Kamianets Podilskiy. It's only about

450 miles from Kyiv yet we wake up in a different world. It's 6.30 am, we don't need to get up yet. I pull the curtain aside. A woman in welly boots, a raincoat and a faded headscarf drives eight cows and a dog along a path beside the railway.

The landscape is dreamlike, a lyric, a poem. Birches are topped with gold. Little haystacks look like golden loaves tipped out of shallow tins.

Our conductor serves us tea bags and hot water in glasses with metal holders. This night ride has cost the equivalent of £4 each.

We've booked into a hotel recommended by a travel bureau in Kyiv. Our taxi driver take us on a roundabout route because no traffic is permitted in the old town. We crane our necks to catch a glimpse of the towers and time-battered walls of the stone fortress that gave Kamianets its name and have acted as a bastion of defence for a thousand years or more.

Our driver acts as an unofficial guide. "Our town is wonderful," he says. "It's historic. Poles and Turks fought here. Are you here for the Festival? Oh, it happens every year. It lasts all weekend, fireworks too. Look, that's the main boulevard . . . we're just coming up to the Military Academy. And look, over there, they're building big houses. We're hard-working people but there's not enough work for everybody."

We unpack and wander into the town. We like old towns and Kamianets doesn't disappoint. Its origins go back into the distant past but the name appears for the first time at the end of the eleventh century. Like Edinburgh with its Old Town and Castle, topography has benefitted the famous fort and the city it guarded. It couldn't have been better situated for defence or for scenic beauty, built high on a rock above a deep ravine with the River Smotrych snaking below. It's a UNESCO heritage site, steeped in history and is rightly called one of the Seven Wonders of Ukraine.

The Mongols destroyed Kamianets Castle in the thirteen century, it rose from the ashes as part of Catholic Poland and, enormously important, defended the Kingdom of Poland from Ottoman and Tatar invasions. All Poland was shocked when in 1672 Ottoman soldiers

KAMIANETS PODILSKIY CASTLE [*PHOTO BY LUMITAR*]

overran Kamianets and changed its churches to mosques. Turkish rule lasted until 1699, when the Castle and the town were returned to the Polish-Lithuanian Commonwealth of Nations. Then Cossack legions swept across the steppe, fighting for independence. It was at this time that the country was first called Ukraine.

A hundred years later, in 1795 Prussia, Austria and Russia seized Poland in a ruthless land grab. Kamianets now belonged to Romanov Russia. Tsarist rule lasted here until 1915. During this time the Castle was used as a prison.

The end of the First World War saw four empires crumble: Prussia, Austria-Hungary, the Ottoman Empire and Tsarist Russia. Kamianets was briefly occupied by soldiers of the newly formed Ukrainian People's Republic until the Bolsheviks seized the town. Battles continued but the Ukrainian independence cause was lost when Soviet Russia swallowed up vast swathes of Ukraine, including Kamianets. The dream of freedom was a thing of the past, protests were put down and whole populations were deported to Siberia and Central Asia. Many died on the way or in the appalling conditions which met them when they arrived in the middle of winter without food or shelter. Soviet rule lasted until Hitler's armies invaded in June 1941. Kamianets suffered great destruction; the Nazis massacred the Jewish population in total secrecy. A Jewish truck driver witnessed the murders and took dangerously illicit photographs, a graphic witness to a monstrous crime.

When the Wehrmacht retreated in 1944, the Red Army took control of the devastated town. An imaginative Soviet architect oversaw the rebuilding of historic buildings. The break-up of the Soviet Union in 1989 finally brought freedom and, eventually, independence to Ukraine, until in 2022 Vladimir Putin decided that the ancient kingdom of Rus' should belong to his autocracy.

This very brief overview of history helps set the scene for this and so many other Ukrainian towns. And having reflected on this background story, Stuart and I head out of town to visit another important castle, Khotyn, it's now a picturesque ruin.

Our mini bus takes us through a part of Europe that time has dealt with variously, often cruelly, but which seems like a rural idyll bathed in the benign light of balmy autumn, though we're already discovering that the economic reality is very different.

Raspberries cling to canes, grapes ripen on arching vines while apples bend the boughs of trees whose trunks have been whitened with lime. Hens who have never heard of battery farms scratch at the roadside. Cottages crowd together. Some are cared for, others have been abandoned.

We pass a newly restored church and a monument to warriors 'who fell fighting fascism.'

And so we reach Khotyn. The imposing ruined castle towers above the River Dnistr. Pigeons flutter around the battlements, jackdaws perch around the tower. It's so peaceful this sunny autumn day that sounds carry from the other side of the wide river. A cock crows, pop music plays in the distance.

We cross a drawbridge and enter the castle. The walls stand firm, stout timber supports an overhanging balcony. Underground dungeons were once used for torture. I prefer the great hall with its wooden roof and the view through glassless windows out to the river, with flat countryside stretching to the horizon.

KHOTYN CASTLE [*PHOTO BY FEDORUK*]

A patch of discoloured stone on one of the walls has given rise to many legends. Could it have been caused by a captive's tears?

It's not surprising that this atmospheric ruin has been used as a setting for many historical films or that novels have been written about the castle and its history. A Polish novelist, Henryk Sienkiewicz (a kind of Sir Walter Scott) wove his novels *The Trilogy* around Polish/Ukrainian events here; popular films based on these books have put Khotyn on the map for generations of readers, viewers and visitors. The leading characters are as familiar as William Wallace, Robert the Bruce and Rob Roy are to Scots.

We've paid a very small fee to view the castle and now go back to the reception area, a simple single storey white building and enjoy a plate of home-made borsht and bread, as well as a chat with the receptionist, Natasha. Her husband had served in the Red Army and she has lived in the Vladivostok region of Russia as well as in West Germany but, she says, Gorbachev swindled them and they lost their savings in a credit crash. A promised house in a good area of Ukraine didn't materialise. Aged thirty three her husband was left with nothing.

The Red Army depended on Ukrainians, she says, and her grandfather, now deceased, witnessed terrible things in the war.

Natasha had worked in Italy for two years to get her daughter through university in Kyiv, her son is in commerce.

We have to be self-sufficient. The Soviets cheated us. I was small when Brezhnev was in power and we had chocolate. You knew you always had food in your cupboard, but now . . .

She brings us home-grown grapes. "My mother makes wine from them and I make juice."

The grapes are small and sweet and aromatic. The skins are tough, they're full of pips but the flavour is – amazing.

"Take them. Look, I'll give you a bag."

We leave Natasha and walk towards the bus stop. A young guy is washing himself down in a bucket of water drawn from a well. Hens cluck and scratch beside him. A cart comes along drawn by two horses, brown and grey. Two girls walk behind the cart while women in headscarves carry heavy shopping bags from a bus stop on the main road. We wait at the roadside. A woman with a fierce-looking dog comes along. "What are you doing here? The bus stop is further up the road."

She presses bunches of grapes into my hand, I savour them as we ride on a crowded bus back to Kamianets. Keats' *Ode to Autumn* sings in my mind. I have just walked right into that poem. I fall completely in love with the sunlit Ukrainian countryside with its 'mellow fruitfulness.'

Back in Kamianets the Old Market Square seems dead. Perhaps everyone is gearing up for the coming Festival. The stiff corpse of a poor expired stray dog is about the liveliest thing in this historic square. But no, here's a swing park with small children on a creaking roundabout.

We have a meal in a hotel: pancakes with mushrooms and sour cream, salad, meat fried in onions and a shared bottle of Ukrainian beer. Russian music plays. The waiter says he works twenty four hour shifts. He's the only waiter in this restaurant which is set up for a wedding with two bridal thrones.

We walk back through the twilight, the gloaming comes so much earlier here than in Edinburgh and the air is still so warm.

Next day an antique-style bar beside the Castle battlements offers lukewarm coffee and nothing else, though three young guys order large pork chops from a bowl which a girl takes from the fridge.

We walk on without the coffee. Women are at work in town, some pull up weeds between paving stones, others sweep up leaves with twig brooms, they all wear orange waistcoats.

Souvenir sellers set out their stalls. We go into a café called *Lilia*. An army veteran with abundant white hair sports a medal-bedecked blazer. He's starting the day with beer and vodka and a heaped plate of food, while young workers drink beer and sup huge bowls of borsht. We get fresh bread, a slice of sausage and a green salad with plastic cups of hot water and a tea bag at the side.

Then, out again into the kindly warmth of the sun, a blessing after grey Edinburgh. We reach the town centre where more stalls are being set up. The Festival is getting into gear, people in period dress begin to throng the streets. We soon realise that this is an international gathering to re-enact historical warfare.

The Ukrainians are here in full Cossack dress, a red waistcoat over an embroidered shirt, baggy trousers tucked into boots. Older men have drooping moustaches, others have the Cossack hair style, shaven heads with a single lock of hair.

There will be mock battles at the Castle later on today. It's good to think that this fortress town is filled with amicable armies, let's hope it stays that way.

Stuart chats in Czech to some guys from Prague who have travelled here for the Festival, other visitors have come from Belarus where these festive war games are an escape from the hardships of life under Lukashenko.

The atmosphere is highly convivial. Beer flows. The festivities will begin tonight and continue tomorrow.

In the tourist bureau we have a choice of guide books, a recently published one in Ukrainian, or one in Polish first published in 1913. We choose the Polish one, which is surprisingly up-to-date because street names which were changed by the Soviets have gone back to their former names. Houses in ruins or needing restored – we trace their story though our guide book.

A stone archway commemorates the visit to Kamianets in 1783 of the last King of Poland, Stanisław August. Twelve years later the unfortunate king had to agree to the illegal land grab by his one-time lover Catherine the Great of Russia, and died a broken man. There's food for thought in the faded lettering on this old archway.

Soviets have ruled here since 1921, the town is still in recovery mode. A woman fills a bucket from a pump and carries it along the road where little cottages are bright with fresh paint.

A bus with school kids pulls up outside a Polish Cathedral. The teacher tells the boys to take off their baseball caps and put them on the girls' heads.

There's a minaret beside the church along with a statue of the Madonna who crowns the sickle moon. The Turks had put up the minaret when they occupied Kamianets in 1672 and when the Poles regained the town almost thirty years later they kept the minaret and put the Heavenly Queen on top. This unusual combination is a bit of a culture shock and now unexpectedly we hear Polish voices. A priest with a typical Roman collar and dark suit calls down from an upstairs window to a colleague. "There are one hundred and thirty nine steps up to the top of the tower," he says in Polish.

He descends, greets us, and, what a coincidence, he remembers Stuart whose work with ecumenical gatherings in Warsaw, thanks to his language skills, was much valued. The priest isn't here for the war games, he has come for a symposium. He gives us a tour round two Polish Catholic churches, one very much under restoration.

Outside in the warm autumn sunshine we come upon Moravians in army outfits, with long hair and cell phones at their waists. Better than guns, I think. They too are here for the Festival.

Our guide book takes along a street of newly-restored, very elegant houses. We read that Jewish merchants once lived there, but there's no plaque to say so.

Kamianets was once an important trading centre. The Armenians brought spices and leather goods, cloth and richly woven carpets, silk, pepper. Armenians prospered, you can still see ornate facades of houses and churches – a bell tower survives. Although foreign, they were accepted; their faith was differently expressed but it was still Christian. Jewish merchants however were often driven outside the city walls by Christian sellers who complained that Jews had unfair advantage with Sunday trade – never mind that from Friday evening until dusk on Saturday no Jewish trade was carried on.

Forced to live by grace and favour of magnates and landowners, Jews acted as tax collectors and rent collectors, toll keepers, money lenders, tavern keepers, water carriers and artisans.

And here we see the roots of deep antipathy which turned neighbours into enemies when Nazi murderers goose-stepped through the towns and villages of Eastern Europe. If a peasant family couldn't pay the rent, if someone got into debt, or even if the beer was weak – well, the Jewish intermediaries were always an easy target to blame and humiliate, rob and murder. With this dark history behind us it's not surprising that we see no obvious signs of Jewish life as we walk around Kamianets.

We explore the famous Castle. It had twelve towers once, only eight remain. The stout walls are pitted with ammunition, while layers of different coloured stone show the rebuilding that has gone on over many centuries, all telling of a stormy past, rich in love affairs, intrigues and spies. We enjoy stunning views from the battlements and then look for an eating place in a quiet part of town. The food is excellent, schnitzel with chips and such fresh tomatoes, all served by a pretty girl in her mid-teens.

I ask to use the toilet. I'm pointed to an outhouse and open the door. Oh dear, the facilities are what you could call basic: a hole in the ground with the inevitable open basket for used toilet paper. However, it's clean and the floor is tiled.

It takes my mind way back to 1965 when I joined a group of ten year old pupils from a Warsaw school for a visit out of town. The little girls and I needed a toilet. There were two wooden ones for public use. We tentatively opened the door – and drew back in disgust. No, this was not for us! I headed a needy delegation to a nearby house and asked if we might use their toilet. The lady of the house looked a bit surprised but took us down the garden where vegetables grew in neat rows – and indicated a hole in the ground. "There," she said and went back inside.

We couldn't quite believe it. The only boy in our group marched forward in true Sarmatian style. "Well, I shall relieve myself."

The little girls and I left dismayed and hoped to find a better facility. At least this Ukrainian convenience is private, not open for all to see.

Later we head for the night train which pulls in an hour before departure time. The passengers who are the most heavily laden go to the front where they will sit up all night on hard seats. Old women drag bags they can hardly carry. A group of four men struggle with a huge load of stuff. Young women arm in arm, tap along on stiletto heels. They are all going to Kyiv with produce to sell, charm not excluded.

Old people who have lived under Stalin, Khrushchev, Brezhnev and Gorbachev with empty promises of a bright future now travel all night in order to survive, hoping that the expense of the long journey will cover its costs and even earn them a little extra. Our travelling companions, Kolya, Oksana and twelve year old Valera tell us all this and more.

Moscow has milked Ukraine, they say. "There were oranges in Moscow," Kolya says. "My uncle worked there, so I knew. I had never seen oranges before."

The family are going to stay with this uncle near Kyiv and will take Valera to the zoo for her thirteenth birthday treat.

They were well travelled: Bulgaria for seaside holidays, Poland to buy a car to sell back home in Ukraine, Prague too and other former Soviet states.

"There's no work in Kamianets." They echo what our taxi driver had told us when we arrived. "All the factories have closed."

They'd tried to start a taxi business but nobody has any money, so business runs at a loss and costs soar.

At a station further down the line Kolya exits the train and returns with an armful of bottles. He gives us one. "It's the very best beer."

It is indeed the very, very best beer. "It's got no additives," he says. "It doesn't keep so you certainly won't see it in a supermarket. It's only brewed here."

Here, is a town called Khmelnytsky after Hetman Bohdan Khmelnytsky, Ukraine's national hero. It's a suitable name as *khmel* means hops in Ukrainian. The great hero's statue is everywhere, there's an enormous one opposite St Sophia's Cathedral in Kyiv.

We settle to sleep but the pillow is bumpy and the mattress is lumpy and the overhead light stays on all night. And it is c-o-l-d!

In fact when we arrive even the crush in the metro doesn't warm us up.

Outside the metro station I buy purple chrysanthemums, plums sweeter than any I've ever tasted. The seller is convinced that I'm Polish. "It's the way you pronounce the Russian words," she says. "I've been to Poland lots of times, so I know."

Stuart laughs, "Well, Jenny, it shows how good your Polish is."

And so it's home to breakfast, to run a hot bath – and sleep.

A child sex slave – beauty and wealth beyond belief

A legendary beauty, Sofia was born in 1760. She grew up knowing three languages, her native Greek, Turkish the language of the country where she was born and Armenian. Soon she would add French. She never fully mastered Ukrainian or Polish but she totally mastered the way to let men master her and give her the wealth and power she dreamt of.

She invented stories of a non-existent titled background in order to charm the highest aristocracy in Ukraine, Poland, France, Austria and Russia. Soon drawing-rooms in major cities were open to her – and so were the beds of counts and kings.

Her mother had sold her when she was in her early teens. The Polish ambassador who bought her was a trickster and deceiver. Dutch in origin, Charles Boscamp had risen in the favour of the Polish king and was ennobled, but he was already beginning to side with the Russians against the king.

Besotted with the beautiful young girl, he taught her French, taught her how to enter and leave a room like a great lady, how to eat elegantly – and how to please a man. He promised not to abandon her when he left for Poland, but failed to honour his promise. Armed with a false genealogy, newly acquired aristocratic manners, with money and jewels that Boscamp had given her and with her new knowledge of the world beyond the coarse talk of the brothel, Sofia set off for the town that Boscamp had mentioned, Kamianets.

The Commander of Kamianets Castle was also of Dutch heritage, Jan de Witte. He mistrusted the young beauty and didn't believe her story, but his son Józef fell in love with her and they married secretly. The father was furious but, according to the novelist Eva Stachniak in her book *The Garden of Venus*, teenage Sofia won the old man over by saying that she would do more for his son and for Kamianets Castle (which she found cold and grey and dreary) than he could ever dream of.

She kept her word. Having heard of her charms, the King himself particularly asked to see her and promoted Józef de Witte to the rank of general.

Soon Sofia was the belle of every ball. No party was complete without the beautiful girl with the enigmatic past. She was in demand everywhere. Marie Antoinette in Paris became a close friend. Sofia, pregnant with Józef's child, still wowed the highest society, she wore loose garments beautifully draped in the classical Greek style. Even the austere, upright and all powerful Habsburg Emperor Joseph was charmed by her.

Sofia and her husband Józef returned to Kamianets with their child, a boy called Jan after his grandfather.

Enriched with money, jewels, and high style, Sofia transformed the Castle into something brighter and more comfortable, but she was fed up with her husband. He was dull, boring and certainly couldn't compete with the royalty who had paid court to her and whose mistress she had become. Józef was now Commander of the all-important Castle and Sofia was the First Lady of the whole region. The King visited her and, perhaps remembering happy intimacies in Warsaw, was godfather to her child.

However, Sofia had set her eyes on the neighbouring estate owned by Count Pototsky, a powerful magnate, one of the richest in the land, owner of many mansions and extensive lands; Sofia had set her heart on becoming Madame la Comtesse. The problem was that there happened to be a Countess Pototska already but that lady's considerable power was no match for the Greek girl's charms. Sofia won the heart of the great Pototsky, first as his mistress and then, having divorced de Witte, as his legally wedded wife, doubly so, because they had two marriage services, a Roman Catholic one and a Greek Orthodox one.

Sofia had been delighted by beautiful gardens she had seen on her travels and her husband had one laid out for her called Sofiyivka after his beloved. The vast garden was said to rival Versailles. Hundreds of trees and plants were brought from far and wide. Sofia loved the garden. Three of her small children were buried there after they had died of smallpox, one after the other. And when her other children, grown to adulthood, distressed her, she took her sorrows to her garden.

Needless to say, Sofia had many other affairs, notably with the powerful and cruel Prince Potemkin, favourite of Catherine the Great of Russia. As his mistress, Sofia, a native Greek speaker who understood and spoke Turkish, was a useful spy during the wars between Russia and Turkey.

Sofia, by then a hugely wealthy widow, died in Berlin, whither she had travelled to seek a cure for advanced cancer. She wanted to be buried in Ukraine, but Prussian bureaucracy made it impossible to transport a dead body across its border, so even in death Madame la Comtesse practised her last deception, all unknown to her. Her married daughters had her body embalmed and dressed in her richest clothes. Heavily veiled and with a fan in one hand and a bouquet of costly fragrant flowers in the other, the corpse was put into a richly caparisoned horse-drawn carriage with her daughters on either side to prop the body up. The hoax worked. Border guards let the stiff, motionless lady through with her entourage and thus the dead body of Sofia travelled back to her adopted homeland where she was finally buried.

Her garden, near Uman, is now both a much visited park and a centre for scientific research – and very recently this quiet backwater, far from any frontline, suffered bombardment and destruction in Putin's war.

One corollary to Sofia's life is that Jan de Witte, the son that she had with Józef, joined the Russian Tsar's notorious secret service and played a part in the arrest of freedom loving dissidents known as the Decembrists in 1826; he also spied on Polish resistance fighters.

As for Charles Boscamp, the man who had owned and groomed the teenage Sofia, he too turned traitor to the Polish cause and in 1794, just before the final partition of Poland, Boscamp was stripped naked and hanged publicly in Warsaw.

Lviv, the City of Lions

It's been called Leopolis, Lwów, Lemberg, Lvov, Львов, and finally Lviv. They say that if you lived here between 1914 and 1946 you could have had six different passports without ever leaving the town, which had passed through the hands of so many different powers, languages and governments in only three decades.

The truth is you probably wouldn't have survived, although amazingly many of the buildings with their mix of High Renaissance, Baroque, Italian, Austrian and Polish architecture have remained relatively unscathed.

The immediate impression is that this city in Western Ukraine is very different from Kyiv. This is because while Tsarist Russia took Kyiv and imposed the feared secret police as well as Russian language, culture and religion on the captured land, Empress Maria Theresa (mother of Maria Antoinette) incorporated Lviv into the Hapsburg Empire. It's said that the Empress didn't like the word 'partition' because it sounded just a little bit illegal and so she made Lviv the capital of a newly formed Kingdom of Galicia and Lodomeria. It's also said that when the deeply pious Empress stole more and more land she "wept as she took, and the more she wept, the more she took".

The Austrian influence has left its mark on Lviv in terms of ambience, architecture and culture, as well as language, and also because the Habsburg regime was less repressive than that of Tsarist Russia.

There are signs of civilisation here from about the fifth century; later too Volodymyr the Great of Kyiv and his son Yaroslav the Wise had their hand in creating a city. However as the power of Kyiv diminished, the whole area came under the control of a Prince called Danylo. Danylo appeased the conquering Mongols, withstood other invaders and unified the western parts of Ukraine, Galicia and Volhynia. He was the real founder of Lviv, and named his city after his son, Lev, which means lion. The City of Lions has kept its name throughout the highs and lows of history.

Not surprisingly Danylo is commemorated in Lviv in a square that bears his name. He's shown on horseback, a truly commanding figure.

The city developed and survived attacks by Turks and Cossacks, Swedes and Russians, it came out of fire, sword and plague still intact, still, as its pre-war motto proclaimed, *Semper fidelis*, always faithful.

Three different archbishops held their seats here: Polish Roman Catholic, Armenian and Greek Catholic (Ukrainian) while Eastern Orthodoxy has its place as well.

A word about the Greek Catholic, or Uniate faith, a union of Eastern Orthodoxy and Roman Catholicism. This Church, which is particularly strong in west Ukraine, has kept the Orthodox liturgy, its feasts and fasts, while acknowledging the Pope. Greek Catholics were severely repressed under the Soviets who viewed their allegiance to the Pope with suspicion.

Scots merchants traded in Lviv. There's still a Scots Café here, which in the 1930s was a notable centre for mathematical discussion, with marble tables set out with pencils for the mathematicians to scribble their results.

Through the centuries of Hapsburg occupation Lviv retained its place as a major cultural centre, with a Ukrainian and a Polish university, although both groups vied with one another for independence. As Habsburg rule drew to a close the city became a centre for Ukrainian calls for independence and for the *Prosvita* (enlightenment) movement which promoted literacy in the Ukrainian language. It was an important centre for Jewish culture too, artists and dramatists worked here, theatre and shows flourished in Yiddish while Jewish students studied in the high schools and colleges. The end came in the Second World War when Nazi policy segregated all Jewish citizens in an area which could only be reached under a railway bridge, the 'bridge of death'. In her book, *Never tell anyone you're Jewish*, Maria Chamberlain, daughter of two Holocaust survivors quotes a letter from her mother written after the war:

> The bridge of death . . . led to Zamarstynowska Street, where the SS picked off scores of Jews who were relocating to the ghetto district . . . 'playing with them' in the most awful way. There they beat children in front of mothers, and mothers in front of children. Nobody then taken came out alive.[6]

Lviv was also undeniably Polish. Aristocrats built luxurious mansions and town houses. The Polish Ossolineum with an enormous collection of Polish books was one of the most important cultural centres in the whole country, especially during the years of the Polish Second Republic (1921-39). Leading Polish writers, dramatists, artists and scientists all worked and studied in Lviv, stamping upon the city a Polish presence that only tyranny and post war politics would eradicate – but not entirely obliterate.

Stuart and I absorb all this as we explore Lviv. We've chosen to stay in the historic Hotel George with its splendid rooms, I've chosen one of the grandest rooms with a palatial bathroom.

The hotel was first built as an inn at the end of the eighteenth century. A local merchant, George Hoffman then converted it into a hotel which is still called after him; the Soviets changed its name and made it an Intourist hotel, equipped with bugged rooms and personnel who reported comings and goings to the KGB.

Now it's known by its original name, Hotel George. Among the guests who stayed were novelists, Honoré Balzac and Henryk Sienkiewicz. For sure Sienkiewicz had read and enjoyed Balzac's novels. I wonder what the French novelist would have thought of the Polish writer's historical epics which are filled with Ukrainian speech and customs.

The Marshal and President of Poland, Józef Piłsudski also stayed in the George, happily a good few years before the Soviet President

---

6   Maria Chamberlain, *Never tell anyone you're Jewish*, Vallentine Mitchell, London 2022, 14.

Leonid Brezhnev. Piłsudski spoke fluent Russian but it's certain that he wouldn't have shared a common language with the Communist Party Leader.

At breakfast we share the dining room with two other guests; both these ladies have stories which mirror something of the complex history of Ukraine.

We speak in English, since both women have lived abroad for many years. They know each other from previous visits here. One lady is a twin. Well, so am I, so that's a common topic of conversation. She shows us photographs of herself and her twin, curly-haired toddlers in pre-war Lviv. This lady is a welcome guest here – her Jewish grandfather had owned the George Hotel.

The other lady has a very different story to tell. Her roots are out in a village. She lives in Canada and can now come openly to Lviv, but it wasn't always so. Her father had been a freedom fighter and, classed by the Soviets as a terrorist, became a wanted and hunted man.

When his daughter first came to Ukraine it was to visit his grave. She tells us how the international flight had landed and armed soldiers immediately approached the exit door. We nod, we've experienced this on visits to USSR in the eighties.

So few international flights touched down in the Soviet bloc in those days that the Lviv airport fence was very low. She could see her cousins and wider family waving from the other side of the fence – they weren't allowed to enter the airport and certainly couldn't visit the hotel where she stayed. The only way they could meet was out in a local park where they knew that they were being followed.

She had tried repeatedly to get permission to go to the village and visit her father's grave. The Intourist official in the hotel always refused. "And you know why," he said. Once she almost succeeded. She hired a car to drive out to the village but the police had got there first; armed men surrounded the entrance to the graveyard, she had to turn back after serious threats. Only with independence did a visit become possible. She will go to the village tomorrow, meet her family and go to the grave.

So, we explore this multi-facetted city where people who once called it home were displaced, while others put down roots and made it theirs.

Hotel George is right in the centre of town, everything is at walking distance, churches, cafés famous for Viennese style coffee and cakes, the art gallery and museums.

[*PHOTO BY TINA KOSTNYUK*]

We survey the grandiose statue of Poland's national poet Adam Mickiewicz. We can't exactly miss this column. Unveiled in 1904, it soars twenty-one metres into the sky, whence has flown a winged female, the Genius of Poetry, who offers the poet a lyre. The statue has survived two world wars and two regimes of terror and we're grateful to Lviv that the Polish Bard, whose best known epic poem begins with longing for his lost native land, is honoured here.

We visit the Lychakivsky graveyard. It's a national museum and an open book into the story of both Polish Lwów and Ukrainian Lviv, into conflicts of the past and the reconciliation of the present.

Gravestones honour Ukrainians and Poles who fought on opposing sides in the fraught year of 1918 when Austria gave Galicia to Ukraine and Poles fought to win it back. So desperate were the Poles to reclaim their Lwów that schoolchildren joined the fighting. They had been reared on Polish patriotism. An ornate tomb in the graveyard honours a professor who wrote a 'catechism for young Polish boys' that every child knew off by heart.

Kim ty jesteś? Polak mały ...

Who are you? A young Pole bright.

What's your sign? An eagle white.

Where do you live? Among my own.

In what land? My Polish home.

How was she won? With sword and blood.

Do you love her? For sure, I should.

For her honour fight and strive;

For her freedom give my life. [*my translation*]

Over two thousand young people, school children and students died fighting to win Lwów for Poland in 1918. The youngest was only nine. And because the Polish coat of arms is an eagle, the young people are called the Polish Eaglets. They were buried alongside defenders of Lviv, both Ukrainians and Poles who first fought against each other, and thereafter fought together against the invading Bolsheviks. Indeed, Poland was the first country to recognise Ukraine as an independent state and the Polish President attended a ceremony when vandalised graves were restored.

We explore the centre of town. Four young guys approach and ask the way. Now, it so often happens that someone asks the way when we're in Warsaw, say, or Barcelona, or St Petersburg. Stuart always knows the answer and the person never guesses that their informant is a foreigner. Stuart has a dictionary and grammar book on one side of his brain and a satnav on the other.

Unfortunately, because we're new to Lviv the satnav hasn't got fully charged. Never mind, we get talking. They have come from Belarus, they say. We tell them that we have friends there and know how awful their life is, how the mother of the family is scared to let her young sons leave the house because shifty shapes haunt the hallway, taking drugs or else are too drunk to stand. The father of this family, a talented blacksmith, used to come to Warsaw to sell his intricate metal work.

Have these young men brought something to sell? "We've come to shout our heads off," they joke, in other words to enjoy freedom of speech in a city that's not controlled by the police.

We think of them as we sit in one of Lviv's many cafés and watch people chatting and enjoying life without having to look over one shoulder to see who might be listening. We think of them too as we visit churches and see people coming and going, lighting a candle and pausing to pray. None of this is state controlled, it's just what people want to do.

Later, we enjoy a concert. The Philharmonia has hosted great musicians through war and peace. The music is always of the highest standard but the concert hall is faded grandeur. Lviv reminds me of an elderly lady, whose elegance is of a bygone era, but whose quality remains beyond doubt.

Stalin's Revenge

A Polish dramatist who lived in Lviv once wrote a light-hearted play, *Zemsta*, Revenge.

Joseph Stalin's revenge was never light-hearted. It was always brutal and murderous, and he exacted his revenge on Polish Lwów in a way that he knew would most hurt.

When Bolshevik armies attacked Warsaw in 1920, Stalin ignored orders from Lenin and detained the invincible Red Cavalry in Lviv. Against all the odds the Poles defeated the Bolsheviks. Lenin and Trotsky blamed the crushing defeat on Stalin's insubordination in keeping the Red Cavalry from the battle lines. Stalin didn't like being in the wrong and never forgave the Poles for this victory. His revenge post-1945 cost Poland its former Eastern Territories, including Polish Lwów.

In 1943, while war still raged, the so-called Big Three: Stalin, an ailing Roosevelt and a war-weary Churchill met in the Russian Tsar's former holiday residence in Yalta where the western leaders gave way to most of Stalin's demands.

The pen being mightier than the sword, these three leaders during their conferences redrew the boundaries of Germany, Poland and Ukraine. What war and terror couldn't do, politicians did. Stalin took all Poland's former Eastern territories, while Ukraine, Latvia, Lithuania, Estonia were incorporated into the Soviet Union, with no possibility of dissent.

Later conferences in Tehran and Potsdam cemented the treaty with not one representative of the countries concerned being present. Shock waves went through the captive lands. Those few lines that realigned the map of Europe caused untold suffering. Heart-broken people, including Polish soldiers who were still fighting in Italy, committed suicide. German families evicted from former East Prussia were also deeply scarred by the trauma they experienced.

Further displacement came in 1946/47. Polish families who remained in the former eastern lands of Ukraine, Belarus and Lithuania were told to leave the homes where their families had lived for generations, where their loved ones were buried and go to Poland. "But this is Poland," simple villagers replied, mystified. "Not any more," they were told. "This is the Soviet Union. If you stay here you'll become Soviet citizens."

Not surprisingly, most left and many took with them a little tin of earth from the eastern homeland they loved. It would be kept for their burial in the new, unknown Poland, formerly Prussia, to which they were now sent in cattle trucks. Some families took a cow or a goat to give them milk on the way.

It was by no means sweetness and light when they arrived. Red tape had to be got through. Newly appointed communist officials despised the barely literate arrivals and gave them a rough time.

It was spooky inside the allocated houses. One man recalls that he and his brothers crawled through deserted German villas and came out with surprising booty: a Mauser pistol, a helmet and a sword. They found nice leather pillows with the words in German 'for a good nap after lunch'. But then they were told that the leather had been made from human skin and the pillows were stuffed with human hair. What should you do with such a pillow when you have no bedding? Throw it away?

It was a shock for families from poor, primitive villages to see the well-built German houses and well laid out farms. Why then had Hitler wanted to steal their lands in the east which were so much poorer, with so little signs of modern living?

Some people entered their new house and found a table set with an unfinished meal, a bowl of soup half drunk and piles of neatly ironed linen in the cupboard.

The biggest surprise came at nightfall when lamps should be lit. A bulb-like object hung from the ceiling, but how could they get it to produce a light? Then the father of the family absent-mindedly put his shoulder against the wall –and a light went on! What strange magic was this? And how could they blow this light out? They would need a ladder or a chair to climb on. Luckily a neighbour came in with an explanation and now the mother kept switching the light on and off, unable to believe that such a wonder was possible in this strange land. She looked round for an icon or a holy picture and found only a book in German, but at least it had a cross on the black cover, they were no longer in the godless USSR, no longer in danger of arrest.

Other unlucky new arrivals, though, had been allocated houses which the Red Army had plundered as they swept westwards. Doors and furniture had been hacked down, duvets and pillows had been torn to shreds in a snowstorm of feathers, electric wires had been pulled out of their sockets and the universal offering of the Red Army, excrement had been left in every room, along with placards in Russian, *Accursed Germans.*

And now that, as Churchill said, an Iron Curtain had fallen across Europe, more displacements took place on both sides of the newly-drawn border between Ukraine and Poland, this was in order to neutralise and eliminate national minorities.

Ethnic Ukrainians were forcibly evicted from the scenic mountainous regions of south east Poland and dispersed among the former German lands in the west. The ostensible reason was to break up groups of

Ukrainian nationalist fighters who carried out guerrilla warfare in the region. Friends and neighbours from tightly knit communities were uprooted and split apart; others were sent into Soviet Ukraine, to coal mines and collective farms while thousands of Ukrainians were deported to Siberia.

Later, in 1997, this forced displacement was rightly described as ethnic cleansing and condemned by both the Polish and Ukrainian governments.

Thus Stalin took his revenge on the freedom loving people of Poland and Ukraine and created countries which were almost entirely free from ethnic minorities.

But although politicians draw lines, history refuses to be totally effaced. Paintwork fades and Yiddish appears. In many parts of Lviv – and elsewhere in Ukraine, we can trace the story that Hitler and Stalin tried to wipe out. Here was a Polish grocery store, there was a Jewish tailor, over there a hat shop. What had been painted over has come back to life and the truth is revealed.

Ukraine, the country at the edge. I leave Stuart in Kyiv and fly home, but 'we're no awa tae bide awa'. Our journey has only just begun.

Travels in Volyn

To capture the essence of a railway journey with a border crossing, go east from Warsaw by night train, Warszawa-Kyiv. At the border between Poland and Ukraine customs officials check documents and wheels are changed to a different gauge. Dawn unfolds across a picturesque landscape. This is Volyn, West Ukraine. Small wooden cottages are surrounded by neat gardens bright with marigolds and autumn flowers. Pumpkins like yellow ochre footballs look as if they'd been tossed over the upturned earth. I can't get over this – I've only ever seen pumpkins in shops.

The sun emerges from the morning mist and shines on yellowing leaves. People cultivate fields in back-breaking ways that haven't changed for centuries. Fields are tilled in the self-same way, hens lay eggs in hard to find places in the self-same way, ducks drink from a pond and a woman leads a goat on a rope. Horses pull long wooden carts, mostly singly, sometimes in pairs. The farmer drives. His wife in her coloured headscarf sits stolidly beside him, while a man chugs by on a motor bike – no crash helmet, of course.

We remind ourselves how this peaceful land was snatched from one neighbouring power to another. While it was still being ruled by the Russian Tsars Germans and Czechs settled here and farmed neat and productive smallholdings. The Czechs, it was said, also brewed the best beer. Armenian merchants brought goods from the exotic east to small towns with mighty castles while cathedrals, monasteries and grammar schools were built by Polish magnates for whom this land had been a bastion against predators from Muscovy and Istanbul, as we saw in Kamianets.

Collectivisation, famine, terror, politics have made this rich past a memory, unmarked, untold, hardly even whispered. Moscow held Ukraine in an iron fist and as a result foreigners are few. Travel is by rail in rolling stock that must surely pre-date even the Stalinist age. All along the line women in orange waistcoats check the passing trains with a yellow flag on an upraised stick. Overcrowded mini-buses connect small towns. Travelling by horse drawn droshky in 1923, two visitors from Wales felt as though they were surfing ocean rollers. The roads don't seem any better now. There is no tourist infra-structure. So why are we travelling here?

Back home in Edinburgh I had discovered a book first published in 1937 and recently reissued. The author, a Polish aristocrat, fluent from earliest childhood in Ukrainian, writes: "And now in front of me lies Krzemienec, a jewel, the most beautiful Polish town . . . It's so beautiful, this Krzemienec, so deeply close to our hearts."

"It's so beautiful . . . the most beautiful Polish town . . ." It's not in Poland any more. The town hasn't moved, it's still in Volyn, north-west Ukraine, but borders have been redrawn and Krzemienec is now called Kremenets.

"Listen to this, the most beautiful town in Poland. We've got to go there," I told Stuart, and so we begin to explore Volyn.

Chapter 2

Volyn

Volhynia – Volyn is one of 25 provinces in Ukraine. Bordering Belarus in the north and Poland in the west, it covers an area of 20,143 square km. A freshwater lake, Svityaz, the largest in Ukraine is a popular resort.

Volyn has changed rulers and languages many times in its long history. It has been overrun by Mongols, has suffered continuous attacks from Tatars, and for many centuries was part of the Lithuanian-Polish Commonwealth. For a while, along with Galicia, Volyn belonged to the Austrian Empire. The weeping Maria Theresa must have shed copious tears when she annexed her share of the territory, but in 1795 Volyn was absorbed into Russia and Poland was erased from the map of Europe. Shocked and horrified a group of Polish luminaries met in Warsaw and decided that "if Poland can't be a political state, we can still be a nation." And the way to do this, they rightly decided, was through language and education.

At about the same time Scotland too experienced a similar fate. Called North Britain and in significant respects subsumed into England – its languages, both Scots and Gaelic were forbidden in the classroom and in public life and were spoken only at home or, in the case of Scots, to raise a laugh in the music hall by the likes of Harry Lauder; laughter, though, that wasn't mocking because the so-called dialect felt comfortable, 'oor ain'.

We are so used to the dominance of English that we seldom think how language and nationhood go together; this lesson is being experienced today in Ukraine as many native Russian speakers switch languages to Ukrainian and change their names accordingly.

There's no direct rail link to Kremenets. Our night train takes us to a major junction, we have three more short train changes ahead. The stations are attractive and clean, with pillars and red tiled roofs, some are still marked by the Soviet red star. Men with black caps pulled over weather-beaten faces carry huge bags. They're most likely going to Lviv or to Warsaw to barter and sell.

The final train on our route has come from Kharkhiv in the east. It's been through Kyiv and is headed for Lviv. People lie on crumpled mattresses in tiers of three bunks the length of a long compartment which seems designed to carry as many passengers as uncomfortably as possible. Having travelled on long distance trains in Russia, I hate to think what the toilet must be like being used by so many people.

We perch on hard seats at the end of the sleeping area. A man beside us tinkers with a broken watch, then pulls a piece of bread out of his pocket, drops a lot of crumbs. He stinks, and the general smell in the wagon has been produced by too many people crowded together after twenty-four hours of travel, with many more hours ahead. It smells of sleep, sweat, bad breath and people's breakfast.

We're glad we're just going one stop, and then we have a short ride on a bus to a town called Dubno where we'll spend a couple of nights. Stuart has found a two star hotel with rooms to spare.

The man at reception tells us that Dubno has 40,000 residents. "Dubno has an important historic complex of buildings, unique in Ukraine," he says and swells with civic pride. I recall a pre-war book that says how beautiful the city looks from afar, a city on a hill surrounded by the meandering river and dominated by the domes and spires of churches and the towers of the castle and a historic gateway.

Our room is three floors up with no lift. It's a good thing we travel light because nobody is on hand to help carry our bags.

The hotel has a restaurant, but it turns out that no food is available because a wedding is expected that evening. No matter! The café right opposite serves coffee for less than forty pence a cup. Huge doughnuts beat anything Western chains can ever offer. Elaborate confections fly off the shelves as mums and grannies indulge sweet-toothed youngsters.

The town centre of Dubno is easily covered on foot. The road is dominated by a fortified gateway which had been built to resist Tatar invaders. Beyond this imposing gateway rises the complex of the cathedral and monastery, buttressed with scaffolding. Under the Soviets this church had been used as a grain store. Although it's still in disrepair, not to say derelict, we notice that there's a bunch of plastic flowers in one of the windows, so we push the door open. A burly chap comes up and proudly shows off the church. He introduces himself. His name is Nikolay, he's an artist and poet and has been working single-handedly to cover the walls with glowing frescoes. Bright colours and huge, naïve figures contrast with the soaring, classical, destroyed décor of the original Roman Catholic cathedral.

Threadbare rugs cover a bumpy, uneven floor. "Archaeologists have been working here," Nikolay explains. He pushes a rug aside and pulls open a trap door. A bishop was buried here, he says and many monks, one on top of the other, nuns too, there had been a convent here as well.

"What happened to their corpses?" I ask, but he doesn't answer, instead he takes us downstairs to the crypt. The dank chill tells its own story.

"This was an NKVD [forerunner of the KGB] prison," Nikolay says and points to memorial wreaths with blue and yellow plastic flowers which have been laid against the far wall of the crypt. He tells us of horrors, skeletons with bound hands and broken teeth, pistol shots in the skulls, bullets embedded in walls so thick that the screams of the victims were unheard in the town.

"Just imagine all that these strong walls have seen and heard," he says.

The Soviets tried to conceal their crimes. They buried the skulls in a field and turned the earth over with tractors. "Skulls tell too much," he explained, "Like how old a person was and how he or she died. They were all fighting for Ukraine to be free. You've heard of Bandera?"

I feel my stomach lurch. Stepan Bandera is the reason why our friends in Warsaw were concerned for our safety when they heard that we planned to travel to Volyn; shocking massacres by Bandera's nationalist party and other right wing groups had taken place there during the Second World War. Their slogan was that every Polish person and all traces of Polish life should be wiped out, so that never again could

Poles claim ownership of this land. Like Bandera, the members of his party had supported the Nazis and had been well tutored in mass murder. The killing spree spread through Volyn and into Galicia. Aided by other right wing groups as well as by local peasants armed with pitchforks, saws and hammers, the murderers raped, mutilated and murdered Polish women and girls, babies were cut in half and children were slaughtered mercilessly. Churches were set on fire with people locked inside, whole villages were razed to the ground and disappeared for ever from the map. Ukrainian villagers who tried to rescue or even warn their friends shared the frightful fate of those they had tried to help.

This is a dark page in the Ukrainian story which in the turmoil of history hasn't been properly examined. Those terrorists who classed themselves as patriots and freedom fighters didn't gain a free independent Ukraine. Instead, their country was controlled by the Kremlin and the KGB who tried to annihilate all traces of Ukrainian nationalism, hence the torture and killings in this crypt. With the fall of Communism, however, Bandera is now classed as a hero of Ukraine with many streets called after him.

Reborn, Ukraine writes its own history, yet I feel uncomfortable down there in that crypt.

"People were severely repressed by the Soviets," says Nikolay. He comes from Ternopil, a town in a region called Podillya and says that in his opinion the Poles had more influence there. The Poles had faith, he says, and some of that has rubbed off on him. The Jews? Well, they were salesmen, business people. Dubno had been mainly Jewish, there were once eighteen synagogues here. In summer the city resounded with kletzmer music, there were Jewish shops and schools.

He gives us a book of his poems.

The priest arrives. He speaks Ukrainian, but understands when we reply in Russian, though Stuart makes a good attempt at the preferred language. The priest is about to go to eastern Poland to sing in Greek Catholic churches there, he gives us a CD, which he dedicates to us, of the all-male choir, all dressed in black.

"Come back and see us. Come back to Ukraine," they both say, and indeed we say this to all our friends, "Come to Ukraine," though we realise that in spite of the fact that everyone is friendly, there's not much help for tourists outside the main cities. Without language, it's not so easy to get around, you need an English speaking guide. Meantime we enjoy coffee and cakes in a café, return to our hotel and sleep soundly, in spite of the wedding.

As I pull back the curtains next morning, I see mist lifting and a rosy sky that promises a good day. There are little houses opposite the hotel and a vista of hills and woodland. The *dub* part of Dubno means oak but I don't know if these trees are oaks or not.

From the height of three floors I look down at a large, clearly significant building. We'll go out and have a look, but first we cross the main road to the café we visited yesterday and enjoy buns, espresso and an excellent leaf tea, then walk round to photograph a splendid but neglected synagogue.

There's no plaque to say what this building once was. Our guide book tells us that it dates from the 16th century, but has undergone renovation, even as recently as the 1980s, although, added the book, there's no-one to use it.

This part of town is truly rural. The imposing synagogue stands among wooden cottages where chickens scratch, cocks crow, dogs bark and a horse pulls a cart of hay. There are bigger houses here too, ruinous, they look as though they had once belonged to important families. I get out my camera to take a picture of an abandoned house. I'm blocking the pavement, a woman asks if she may pass and we get talking. She has only lived in Dubno for two years, she says, before that she lived in a village. She misses her garden, her rabbits and her cow, but she's had an operation and her health is not so good. Her children don't like country life, so she's moved into town.

She wonders why I'm taking so many pictures. "It's people who beautify a town, not buildings." And just then one of Dubno's beauties taps by on impossibly high heels. Her boots, decorated up the sides with gold, would certainly grace a photograph.

Another abandoned house cries out for renovation. A crumbling brick gable rises above the faded yellow ochre paint of its walls. Ornate edgings are picked out in white, faded now to grey. Did a well-to-do merchant family live here? Lettering, partly obliterated, indicates that there was once a workshop here with goods of proven quality.

We wander on through the town and take more photographs in spite of the lady's admonishments. A Roman Catholic parish church indicates a Polish presence. It's an austere building in need of some refurbishment. Two white pillars support the doorway. A man approaches. He reeks of booze and nurses a broken arm. "I live here," he keeps repeating and tells us that there are regular services with about fifty people attending.

A lorry is parked so that the driver's cab juts out into the main road. It blocks a green Lada car and a crowded bus with four gas canisters on the roof. Overtaking them at a gallop, a cart rattles away from market pulled by two lean horses. Their chestnut coats gleam like conkers in the sun.

Young people cluster outside a pub. Families are returning from a walk beside the river, so we go in that direction. A bridge leads to woods, once the parkland of a grand palace. Here, in a scene that could have been painted by an eighteenth century landscape artist like Alexander Naismith, a small boy casts his rod hopefully into the river, a goat grazes and a tanned young man digs the rich dark earth of a sizeable garden which slopes steeply down towards the river. Cottages stand in a row along the bank. One boasts a satellite television dish and by way of stark contrast a man fills a pail at a communal pump.

We find a café on the river bank where we both enjoy a salad. Stuart orders a meat mixture which comes in an earthenware dish along with potatoes; I have fish served with herbs and chips. We choose a bottle of Moldovan red wine. The girl who serves us has a bit of a struggle to understand Russian, it's no longer compulsory in the new Ukraine. She's a wee country lass. She has a room in an apartment in Dubno. Another girl comes out from the kitchen to join the chat. Yes, people not buildings beautify a town and you meet them when you go freelance. You maybe miss a lot of touristic sights, but you gain insights into the way people live.

We cross over a bridge to the ruined castle which, built on a rocky outcrop, towers over the peaceful water of the river. It dates back to the 15th century and has changed owners over the years. Devastated in the First World War, the castle now attracts tourists from Ukraine and even further afield. There are two tour buses parked outside. One is ramshackle from the Soviet era. It has brought schoolchildren from the next town on our journey, Kremenets. The other bus is swish and modern and the tour guide speaks to this group in English.

The rooms are devoid of furnishings but photographs around the walls show how palatial it once was. The aristocratic family who inherited the totally devastated castle in 1920 restored it completely, but then lost it when the Soviets invaded West Ukraine in 1939.

The present restoration is a joint Ukrainian-Polish venture, it's good to see the blue and yellow and red and white ribbons side by side, but for Polish people the loss of these lands has left a scar. It has faded with the passing of time, partly because of propaganda which tried to sell the re-drawn map of post-war Poland, but the memory of the Volyn genocide is still very real. "The Polish-Ukrainian story is one of bloodshed," a young woman in Edinburgh said just the other day when I told her about this book.

Armies come and go but apple trees still grow in the abandoned gardens. We gather windfalls and enjoy them.

As dusk deepens and street lights come on, young people meet up in front of a bar. It looks expensive, newly built in a traditional style to blend with the red brick battlements of the castle. The blue and red tent of a circus strikes a cheerful note, although the circus doesn't seem to be in operation at the moment.

We go back to our hotel. Tomorrow we'll be on our way to Kremenets.

Kremenets, a town off the beaten track

We arrive by bus – the railway doesn't run to Kremenets. The ticket office is a former *shul*, or Jewish study centre. A shiver passes through me as I look the distinctive architecture and realise that the empty space around the bus terminus was once a thriving centre. I've seen pre-war photographs of Kremenets that show signs in Yiddish and Polish which tell you that you can get your boots mended by the Jewish cobbler and your best coat expertly altered by the Jewish tailor, or you can get your teeth sorted at Sheinberg the dentist's, your hair done at Madame Bluma's, while your joinery will be looked after by Mr Rosenfeld.

Empty spaces in Ukrainian towns so often tell a silent story. I shall fill this particular space with a few names gleaned from my researches.

In 1934 members of a Jewish organisation asked the mayor of Kremenets for permission to open a local branch. Their names and addresses, in Polish, were:

Gersz Kac, 7 Baupré Street, born in 1894

Gersz Rubinfein, 44 Słowacki Street, born in 1904

Motel Feld, 19 Szeroka Street, born 1893

Szmuel Orzech 23/4 Dubieńska Street

Szaja Bezpojaśnik, 29 Franciszkańska Street

Jefim Szyfris, 179 Szeroka Street, born 1901

Abram Trachtenberg, 66 Szeroka Street, born 1901

Segal Nisan Direktorska Street, born 1907

I can only guess their fates.

Kremenets is all up or down. It is cut through by a main road up which buses struggle, belching exhaust fumes. Cars are few, but the driving is dangerous. The long road which leads through Kremenets is now called Shevchenko Street. Before the war it was called Szeroka Street – Wide Street, mentioned in the addresses above.

We leave our bags in a room in a small hotel and follow the road uphill into the centre of town, a steady but gentle slope for one and a half kilometres. Ahead are the domes of Orthodox churches, one, sparkling green and gold is a now a convent. We come to an empty space with a Soviet war memorial, beyond that is a huge architectural ensemble crowned by a large Baroque church. An imposing building houses a teacher training college and a centre for the humanities, music and dance. It's dedicated to the Ukrainian national poet, Taras Shevchenko (1814-1861). Here are the first and last verses of his poem, *Testament*:

When I die, dig my grave
high on the broad steppes of my dear Ukraine
so that I shall see the boundless plain
and steep banks of the Dnipro
and hear how the river roars . . .
Bury me and arise,
break your shackles and sprinkle your freedom
with the evil blood of the enemy;
and in the new great family of the free
remember me with a kindly word. [*translated by Stuart and Jenny*]

Ah, Freedom is indeed a noble thing . . . There are two narratives in Kremenets, and two acts of memory, for on the archway are two Polish names: Tadeusz Czacki and Hugo Kołłątaj.

And now I must go right back to the time when I began to study Polish.

I soon found myself in a fog of incomprehension. Nouns were unlike any language I'd come across, there are seven ways of saying 'you' – how impoverished English is with only one, what nuances of relationships we miss! And you use the verb 'to go' in so many different ways in Polish, depending whether you walk or take some means of transport and how often you perform the activity. "You know," Stuart says, "the verbs of motion on the right hand column in the grammar book."

No, I don't know. I prefer poetry to grammar books. The problem is, you can't learn a language without grammar.

Yet in this confusion two facts got fixed in my mind. I had always thought that the Armistice in 1918 had meant the end of war. I now learnt that for Poland it was only the beginning of another war to regain lost lands in the east. And a name stuck in my mind, a complicated name, Kołłątaj. I learnt that this name was associated with education.

So here I am in Kremenets, which was once called Krzemieniec and these two facts fall into place like pieces in a jigsaw.

Alarmed that, in 1795 with the final Partition of Poland, Polish was in danger of becoming a private language used, like Gaelic, only at home or between friends, a committee in Warsaw set themselves up as the Commission for National Education. Out of their meetings came the idea of founding a Lyceum, a college on par with a university. The main instigator was Tadeusz Czacki, a self-taught man of huge erudition. Help came from a surprising source, Tsar Alexander l, who wanted to bring educational reform to his vast empire. Czacki seized this unexpected window of opportunity. Backed up by a fellow reformer, Canon Hugo Kołłątaj, the High School or Lyceum was established, a true jewel in an obliterated stately crown.

The location was deliberately chosen. The reformers wanted a town well off the beaten track. There was no army garrison there, so no heavy drinking or visits to houses of pleasure to distract young students. If the quiet Volyn town created the great study centre, the Lyceum in its turn made Kremenets 'the most beautiful Polish town.' It attracted the cream of promising boyhood and their families. Villas and town houses were built around the Baroque churches. Leading academics flocked to the sleepy town, set so beautifully among hills and woodland and deep valleys. The Lyceum soon produced distinguished scholars, poets and social activists. Juliusz Słowacki, one of the greatest Romantic poets, was born here.

But then, alarmed at the blossoming of language and of freedom of thought that produced demands for freedom of statehood, Tsar Alexander reneged on his reforms, closed the Lyceum and had its precious collection of books taken to Kyiv, firmly under Tsarist control.

When Poland regained its freedom and had its borders recognised in 1921 at the cost of burgeoning, but suppressed, Ukrainian independence, the Lyceum became an important educational centre once more. Under an enlightened regional governor who supported Ukrainian demands for more autonomy, Ukrainian schools were opened, but in the 1930s Polish politics became increasingly nationalistic and illiberal.

So much for background. Let's explore this former jewel. It's good to see that Czacki's vision and hard work haven't been in vain because this teacher training college draws students from far and wide. Education still flourishes in Kremenets and a cultural sharing has been in evidence since 1991 when Poland was the first country to recognise Ukrainian independence.

With this shared inheritance in mind, we ask the way to the Juliusz Słowacki Museum. Local people misdirect us twice but we enjoy our wander around the back streets and gardens of Kremenets on our way to the restored house which had belonged to the poet's grandparents, it's now used for cultural events.

In the terrible year of 1939 there were plans to hold an exhibition of the work of Juliusz Słowacki on the anniversary of his birthday, 4th September. Instead as the German blitzkrieg blasted Poland all the artefacts were hastily moved from the house. The Polish people of Krzemieniec who survived deportation to the depths of the USSR, mass murder at home and exile in Britain, Canada, and elsewhere, never forgot the town they loved or its poet who had left his words in their hearts. They contributed to the renovation of the house.

The custodian is pleased to show us round and takes us up to the botanic gardens which had been an important part of the education of the Lyceum. It's quite a climb up and a long walk round the extensive gardens, so I'm glad to head back downhill and find somewhere to eat.

We settle on a place called *At Ludmila's* where we sit outside in the late afternoon sun and enjoy a local delicacy, a spicy soup with beans and potatoes, along with a salad and tasty bread.

Our view of the main road is restricted by an elaborate metal fence, but a stray cat and a group of ownerless dogs keep us company until somebody chases them away. They are sad, these dogs, not vicious, definitely not to be fed from the table or patted or spoken to – and always a sign of a broken infrastructure.

Through the metal work we see the occasional vehicle drive past and watch the passers-by: young women in miniskirts strut their stuff on impossibly high stiletto heels, while old women in headscarves hobble along to church.

We top up our meal with coffee and head for our hotel. It's a golden autumn day with gorgeous views over sunlit woodland and distant hills. Pine trees stretch up a hillside towards a majestic ruined castle, picture postcard material and visible from all over the town. A formidable Italian queen, Bona, married to a Polish king in the fifteenth century, had the castle constructed so strongly that it finally took an act of treachery to destroy it. Bona brought wealth and security to her new kingdom, she founded convents and churches, introduced Renaissance thought and architecture – as well as lettuce, cauliflower, asparagus, carrots and celery.

The ruined castle is on the local tourist trail, while the hillsides around Kremenets make it a popular centre for long walks in summer and winter sports, yet the town barely gets a mention in my English language guide book. Coach tours tend to stay in a motel outside the Kremenets, many drive straight through the town to visit an ancient site of prayer and pilgrimage, the Orthodox monastery of the Dormition, the Pochayiv Lavra.

The air is fresh, the countryside is gentle. People are hospitable and kindly. Before the war this was a favourite resort. Families came in horse drawn charabancs to stay in residences among the health giving pines. There were pleasant guest houses and a lively cultural life, thanks to the prestigious Lyceum. We're glad that young people still study in its splendid buildings, but international tourists are few. Yet there are groups of elderly people in Poland, Canada and Israel who still preserve the memory of the vibrant town of their childhood which was known as the Athens of Volhynia.

Our small hotel, when we reach it, is occupied by Russian businessmen, tourists of a different sort. The Russian guests leave and return with local women in tow. Their audible pleasure lasts well into the next morning. The cleaning lady laughs, "Lucky for some!" She kindly gives us a kettle, a plate and a bread knife.

It's cold in our room. "It's snowing in America," the cleaner says helpfully. "And besides, it's *Pokrov*." This feast of the Protecting Veil marks the end of autumn and beginning of winter. People say, "If it snows at *Pokrov*, it will snow all winter."

I pile on as many layers of clothes as I can find and we emerge into a cold, damp morning. A stray dog has been run over. A woman lifts it by the tail and carries it off the main road.

It's Sunday. People are leaving a service in a historic church, now under restoration. A man unrolls a patterned carpet. He's very affable and draws a map to show us the way to cemetery where the poet Słowacki's mother is buried. A lady in a headscarf speaks to us in a mixture of Russian and Ukrainian. "There's going to be a wedding later today," she says, as she guides us through the building. "All this restoration is home-grown, the parishioners are doing it themselves, although the Patriarch gave $200."

Following the instructions from our two friendly guides, we head up a side road and slither over muddy cobbles, it has rained in the night. There's a smell of horse dung and apples, windfalls from a tall tree. A woman who carries a large bunch of flowers from her garden greets us and confirms that we're on the right road.

The dead lie among quiet trees and piles of flowers. Names, dates and their portraits tell their story. Wooden crosses are draped with traditional embroidered linen. The mother of the poet Juliusz Słowacki is honoured with a stone memorial. Plastic flowers are scattered around the marble steps, the poet's maternal grandparents are buried close by.

As we walk back through the town we see sad signs of neglect. Houses that had once been grand villas are run down. An ornate metal balcony with delicate Art Nouveau designs has no base, another literally hangs off the wall. Little cottages look as if they're about to collapse into the ground while peeling paintwork shows plasterwork and bare bricks.

Remember, again, I'm writing this before Putin's invasion and the appalling destruction of so many cities in Ukraine which make a hanging balcony and a bit of bare brickwork seem ridiculously negligible.

We go back to Ludmila's for lunch. Today we have salads made with shredded cabbage and tomatoes topped with sour cream, bread, not as fresh as yesterday's, then *pelmeny*, little round dumplings stuffed with meat, and *vareniky*, which are similar but with mushrooms. Stuart drinks beer with the meal. I'm not keen and don't like mineral water either, so I have tea. We finish with coffee – and all this food comes at such low prices that eating out is highly affordable.

Chef hands homemade vareniky [*photo by Milkas*]

The toilet requires a bit of gymnastics. I have to mount a step and then squat. Soiled paper goes into an open bin, along with cigarette butts and other rubbish. It's clean but not a place to linger in. There's a tap and a wonky dryer that makes a lot of noise but gives a poor result.

Well fuelled, we seek the historic Polish cemetery which is situated near the town park – another empty space; it had been a ghetto during the war, the lady in church had told us. My later reading tells me that there had been an uprising here, pre-dating the Warsaw Ghetto Uprising. The Jewish community was totally wiped out, those few who survived had done so by escaping into Soviet Ukraine across the closely guarded border.

A stone wall and archway leads us into the Polish graveyard. The archway commemorates teachers and leading townspeople who had been murdered in 1942. We pause to read their names, then walk uphill past graves that had been abandoned long ago.

You may wonder, why go into graveyards? Well, so often the gravestones are like pages of a family album. They tell us who these people and their families were, even what their jobs were. We can build up a picture of a whole community, and today, it turns out, we have a guide. A couple who are visiting from London have enlisted a local woman's help in finding a family grave. This local lady is Polish by birth, she has lived in Kremenets all her life. She's wearing a waterproof jacket, strong laced boots and a bright red beret pulled firmly over her white hair. She takes us uphill to her mother's grave. She's paid for a tombstone to be erected but the cement is still damp, frost has been forecast, she wants to protect the cement with pieces of sacking which we help her lay in place and cover with a thick polythene sheet. She tells us that she and her son do their best to tend the graves, to pull back abundant vegetation which soon grows back again.

"They wanted to take this historic cemetery from us and make it into a park, but it's so difficult to maintain it. Just look at these beautiful monuments all overgrown, so you can't make them out any more. Now excuse me . . ."

And Maria in her distinctive regional accent recites prayers at her mother's grave before she continues our tour. "See that mound over there with the wooden cross? We parishioners put that up for our priest. He served us when times were hard."

"How was it for you, growing up here after the war as a Pole in a Ukrainian town?"

"Hard," she says. "My father went to Poland and never came back. I was in the seventh class (about twelve years old) before I got my first pair of shoes . . . Yes, very hard. I got called derogatory names. Now, see here, look at that grave. They were all murdered, the whole family, all on the same day. The little one was just a year old."

Maria is referring to the brutal murders carried out against Polish villagers by Ukrainian nationalists and even by former friends and neighbours in 1943 – 44. We can understand that it was indeed hard for Maria and the small Polish remnant left in Volyn to grow up as aliens in their own land, their language spoken only at home until it too dies away from lack of use.

Maria works as a guide and offers to take us by taxi up to the ruined castle built by Queen Bona.

The wind is cold but as the taxi climbs up a paved winding road we see that the clouds have lifted, giving us views over a wide plain.

The castle was invincible, says Maria. Cossack armies besieged it in 1648 but couldn't gain entrance until, through treachery, a door was opened and someone let the besiegers in. Fierce battles raged around the castle for another six weeks until it was destroyed, leaving only a semi-circle of stones; walls of double thickness and an archway that still crowns the hill.

A tethered cow grazes among the ruins. Two children appear from nowhere, a girl and a boy. They offer me round black stones, "to purify the water," they say. "Thank you," I say in Ukrainian. "Now give us a *złotówka*," they beg in broken Polish, naming the Polish currency – they're obviously well used to tourists.

We should, Maria says, be able to see the golden domes of the Pochayiv Lavra, but it's still too dull. "You've come so late in the year," she says. "You should come in spring when the leaves unfurl. Ah, summer, you should come here then!"

"How about winter? Is there much snow?"

"Oh, yes, two years ago, what a lot of snow! I said to my mother – she was still alive then, never mind, this is the first fall of snow, it will melt by tomorrow. How wrong I was! It lasted until March. Now, come, there's someone I want you to meet."

The car negotiates a hairpin bend and bumps back down the hill. We pay the driver and walk pass wooden cottages with gardens bright with marigolds, Michaelmas daisies and chrysanthemums. Neighbours greet Maria who then knocks on a front door. The man whom we had met up at the graveyard along with his wife, opens the door and takes us down the hall. The door on the left leads to a room where an elderly lady, Pani (Madame) Irena Sandecka is eating a plate of soup. There are holy pictures on the wall, including one of Pope John Paul II. Pani Irena is 94 and still colours her fuzz of curls, her eyes are bright. She has no front teeth, wears amber beads and a small Scout badge.

"She has no lavatory or bath," Maria whispers and adds, "That's our reality, it's the way we live." She has already told us that she and her husband, an engineer, have a pension of $74 per month. She would like to give us her address so that if we know of any tourist groups that might come here, she could be their guide.

Pani Irena was born in Uman in 1912. It became Soviet when she was eleven and her parents decided to cross the border illegally into free Poland. They came to Kremenets where Irena's mother taught Polish in the newly opened Lyceum. So Irena studied there, stayed on to do teacher training and then, in 1931 did further studies in the prestigious Jagiellonian University in Kraków. Thereafter she became a teacher of Polish back in Kremenets. Always socially active and a keen member of Polish Scouting, Irena travelled to Belgium in the summer of 1939. She planned to run Scouting activities and Polish classes for the children of emigrant workers in industrial centres. The outbreak of war put paid to these plans. Irena returned to Poland. Thousands of others, including the Polish government, were escaping westwards, but she went the other way. She travelled through France, Switzerland, Italy, Hungary and Romania right home to Kremenets which was now under Soviet occupation.

Irena immediately got in touch with a Polish underground group and later, under German occupation, organised help for Polish villagers who had fled to Kremenets from nationalist attacks. It was safer in town than in the country during that genocide. Although the German armies actively encouraged the murderers and offered no support to their victims, the head of the German garrison stationed in Kremenets actually helped Irena get papers and transport for the refugees. She herself managed to rescue ninety orphans and took them to Kraków to safety.

When the Soviets retook Kremenets and forced so-called 'repatriation' programmes on Polish citizens, Irena refused to leave. She trained as a laboratory assistant but the main thrust of her life was to resist the Soviets and work on behalf of Polish families who had stayed in Communist Ukraine.

An ardent Catholic, she managed to maintain the church during the harshest Soviet repression – the only Roman Catholic Church that was open in all Volyn.

"Have you seen it yet? Oh, you should! It's modelled on our famous St Catherine's Church in St Petersburg. Of course the Communists closed that church after 1917, but here we had a secret weapon."

"God?" we wonder. "Or the Virgin?"

No, the poet Juliusz Słowacki. A large bronze relief of the poet had been smuggled to Kremenets in 1909 and mounted on marble inside the church. It was the work of the sculptor who had made the better known monument to the composer Chopin in Warsaw and it was always much visited, to the surprise of local Soviet functionaries.

"Who is this poet that so many tourists come to see?" they asked Irena.

"Don't you know? He's a famous revolutionary," Irena told him.

So thanks to the 'revolutionary' poet the church was saved. Irena organised teams of helpers to clean and care for the building while she played the organ, gave children secret lessons and prepared them for Holy Communion. The KGB stopped her, so she took classes secretly with never more than three children present. Any more, she was told, would be a group meeting and that was forbidden.

Eventually after Stalin's death, priests began to come to the church to hold services in secret. She had them stay with her, a highly dangerous act of hospitality.

Irena has become an institution in her own right. The Communist President of Poland interviewed her on Polish Television and Maria tells us that even in her eighties Irena took visitors up to the ruined castle.

"She bounded up the hill like a teenager," Maria says and indeed she's truly impressive: her bright spirit – and her extreme poverty. A puff of wind would blow her flimsy hut away.

"I'm happy. I have my pension, my books. And I have my garden . . ."
And cats, we think, for the place smells too strongly of them.

She keeps pressing hospitality on us: salted straws, sweets and apple juice that tastes decidedly fermented. She's pleased that two Scots have come to Kremenets. "This must be the first time," she says, but we've read that the young Słowacki's tutor was called William James MacDonald, so maybe there were Scots in Kremenets long before us.

We rise stiff and cold from Irena's table and decide to walk back to our hotel.

"It's more than two kilometres," Maria objects, but I need to walk off the smell of incontinence, of cats and poverty, and also to process what we have seen and heard. A picture remains with me. Irena had told us that during her interviews in Communist Poland she had been told never to mention the Volyn murders that she had personally witnessed. She had seen a woman lying beheaded with a murdered child beside her, a little boy, perhaps four years old; long lashes covered his closed eyes. "His Mummy must have told him to close his eyes." There was a long red gash across his throat.

"There can never be justice in Poland or Ukraine until these murders are acknowledged." Irena had said.

She died in 2010 aged ninety eight, a remarkable woman who had already become a legend during her long lifetime.

Back at the hotel we discover that the amorous Russians and their happy partners have gone, so we have a quiet night and next day set out once more in sunny – if cool – autumn weather to explore more of Kremenets.

Our walk takes us uphill through woodland, oaks, beeches, rich in gold. It's a stiff climb. Stuart's knee is bad and we find strong sticks to help us along, never guessing we'll cause mayhem when we dip back down through the woods towards some cottages. Dogs announce our arrival and an old lady hobbles out of her garden. "What's this? They're coming with sticks to beat us!"

A couple of men come out to see what the fuss is about. They can't understand what two foreigners are doing here, after all we don't have any relatives in the town. The younger man tells us he's been to Poland to work. Stuart, friend of all the world, opens up the conversation. He throws in as much Ukrainian as he can muster. There's laughter and lots of goodwill.

"The air's so fresh," I manage.

"We've got good water too," the older man says. "*Baba* (old woman) will show you our well. Speak Russian," he tells her for our benefit.

"I can't speak Russian," she says, but as she takes us along a muddy path she pours out her story.

"My older brother got taken away to concentration camp. I was ten. We never saw him again. What's it like in winter? Lots of snow, we're used to it. I'm all alone here. I worked in a factory. The Soviets took everything."

She has two headscarves bound tightly about her head, an overall and a pinafore. She wears rubber boots and walks with a purposeful step. Small children in welly boots play in the garden close by. Their mother has been for water, she's carrying two buckets on a wooden yoke across her shoulders.

The old lady too walks this way up and down muddy trails, through snow and ice with a yoke and buckets. "We do our washing in the well," she says. She rinses the washing in pure, clear water which flows through a pipe straight out of the hillside. I imagine how cold the water must be in winter, how frozen her hands.

A wooden cross with an icon of the Baptism of Christ stands by the well. It's decorated with the traditional embroidered linen cloth and the ubiquitous plastic flowers. "We bless the well. Water is sacred," the elderly lady says as she keeps her mouth grimly shut. She has only one tooth. "My daughter tells me to put my teeth in but I always forget."

Her daughter works in Kyiv and never visits. It's too far, too expensive, she's got no time.

Baba wants us to linger, bids a warm farewell and sets us on our way to the Jewish cemetery. We go down *Dzherelo* (well or spring) Street, a good name for this stony road which leads from the well. From there it's a hike along another trail and up a steep hill to get to the historic, abandoned Jewish cemetery. Our guide book tells us that this is one of the oldest and largest Jewish graveyards in Volyn with more than a thousand graves. Broken stones cluster together, others that look more like rocks are scattered far and wide across the overgrown hillside. It's sad to see this abandoned graveyard, such a record of a vibrant community over many centuries. We don't know if there are any Jewish people left in Kremenets. Somebody told us that there are two families here, but this was disputed. It seems very unlikely.

We walk back to town for coffee and chat to a student who tells us that she's come from her home town to do a course in the teacher training institute here to become a nursery teacher. Then we set off on further exploration and head off away from town. An old lady pauses to greet us. She is delighted to talk so we walk with her at her pace. She's wearing the inevitable head scarf and slippers whose toes have burst through.

"I like to walk," she says. "It's so good for me."

She's carrying an empty bag and obviously isn't heading for the shops. Of course, mushrooms!

There's the sound of wheels and the steady clip clop of horses. A cart drawn by two horses trundles by and leaves that distinctive horse smell.

The lady lives in an apartment block in town with her children and grandchildren. "I love my family and they love me." She's amazed that we've spent the equivalent of £10 for our stay in the hotel – she probably doesn't see that amount of money in a month.

She was born in 1935, she tells us. There were eight of us in the family, she says. One brother never came back from the war, another died young, a sister died too. She counts them off on her broad, hard-working fingers.

"I remember when Polish families lived here, a mother and daughter. Then the aeroplanes came, they dropped bombs. The little girl was so scared that she hid under the bushes. Then they left. I don't know where they went. They gave us a table and chairs and some dishes. We were very poor. My father had no land. He was a carpenter."

She remember the Jews too, they used to carry wood in rucksacks on their backs.

She points out raspberry bushes and wants to give us some berries, but it's too late in the year, she's disappointed that she can't offer us anything.

She asks about life in our country. We find it hard to know what to say. Ours is such a different world from this lovely countryside, the silence and fresh air.

"I am poor," she says. "But I am content."

And yes, you can see it in her clear blue eyes, a deep peace.

"Are you staying long? There will be a big church festival to celebrate *Pokrov*. My mother and auntie always said that if there's a cold wind on *Pokrov* it will be cold all winter. I remembered their words one winter when a warm wind blew, and right enough, we had a warm winter."

By now we've reached the main road. She doesn't want to say goodbye. Having learnt that Stuart is a priest she asks him to bless her. She cups her folded hands to receive the blessing and we part.

This road takes us to a village, another steep walk. A man, along with his wife and daughter who are working in a field, look at us suspiciously, they're clearly not used to strangers. We pass houses and a church, freshly painted in white, with a single dome. Two children are gathering mushrooms. The little boy has a dangerously sharp knife. He holds up three fingers to show how old he is. I talk to them in Russian, they understand, but answer in Ukrainian. Clever wee souls, bi-lingual so young! Meantime Stuart is chatting to a village woman. These are the priest's children, she says, as an older girl runs up from the house beside the church. The woman tells us that there's a bus to Kremenets from here, but we walk on towards the town and fill our water bottle at a pipe where clear water pours out from a stream.

A boy rides a bike over the steep, rutted track. His sister pastures a cow. We talk to a family who are unloading vegetables from their cart. They all talk at once, and tell us that village is called Zholoby, the name goes back to the Cossacks, the father of the family says. "You should go and visit the Cossack graves in town."

Stuart comments on the mountain of beets. "You'll make a lot of soup," he says and they roar with laughter. "It's not for us, it's for the cattle," the man laughs.

Back in town we refuel with a late lunch and look for the third cemetery of our visit. Once again we're misdirected, this time by a man who tells us that he's a Pentecostal Christian. He was converted in prison. His hands are black with oil, there's a finger missing. He's mending a lorry parked by his house. A young man called Vitya comes out. "I'll take you. It's good that you understand Ukrainian."

He heads along another steep path at breakneck speed. "Am I going too fast?"

Church bells jangle from the town at 5 pm, the carillon lasts half an hour and will be repeated at 3am in honour of Pokrov. The clamour sets dogs barking. It could bring a court case for noise pollution further west, I reflect.

Vitya makes wooden doors for a living. He hopes we'll buy shrubs he's growing in tubs outside his garden.

A bus pulls up and a man and woman get off, they're laden with pails of mushrooms they've come here to sell.

Vitya walks on at his quick pace to a hillside cemetery where Cossack graves are marked with small stone crosses that crouch low in the long grass. One grave has Cyrillic lettering which is still visible, another with ornate carvings is honoured with a traditional embroidered cloth and plastic wreath. Vitya explains that these graves probably date back a good few hundred years, perhaps to 1648 when the Cossacks besieged the mighty castle. A modern sandstone mural depicts a couple of Cossack men with their distinctive coiffure, shaven head and a single quiff of hair. A freedom-loving 'Braveheart' warrior stands beside a minstrel with a *bandura*, the traditional Cossack stringed instrument, not to be confused with the surname Bandera.

We thank Vitya for guiding us here, he takes us all the way back to the centre of town, even though we haven't bought his shrubs.

Cossacks

All right, who are the Cossacks who have already cropped up in our story? We met them dressed for pretend battle in the mock war games at Kamianets.

We can go far back in time to look for the ethnic origins of the people who became known as Cossacks, but let's go to the vast grasslands of the Ukrainian steppe, the so called 'Wild Fields.' The demand for grain and cereals from the rich soil of Ukraine led to these fertile lands being valued for trade. The people who moved there in search of wealth and freedom often became victims of Tatar slaving raids to be sold in the Ottoman Empire where children and young people fetched the highest prices. And now the Cossacks become a fighting force who attacked both the Tatars and the Turks, set the captives free and went down in folklore as heroes.

The first Cossacks, the name is Turkish, were adventurers, traders, runaways, warriors.

Some are hiding from paternal authority, or from slavery, or from service, or from [punishment for] crimes or from debts or from something else; others are attracted [to the region], especially in spring, by richer game and more plentiful places. And, having tried their luck in its fortresses, they never come back from there.[1]

As Cossack raids became ever more frequent, kings and princes were glad to have the fiercest fighters on side as guards and officers in their armies. Some Cossacks later became loyal guards for the Romanov Tsars. Renowned horsemen, they could perform remarkable feats on horseback. Their local communities under fiery charismatic leaders fought fiercely for an independent Ukraine. One of their main branches was in a region very much in the news of Putin's war: Zaporizhzhia.

In the seventeenth century the Cossacks of Zaporizhzhia banded together to fight for a free independent Ukraine under their leader, Bohdan Khmelnitsky. Khmelnitsky sought revenge on a Polish magnate who had stolen his lands and killed his son. With Tatar and Ottoman

---

1   Michalon the Lithuanian, quoted in Serhii Plokhy, *The Gates of Europe*, London 2016, 76, 77. See chapter 7 for more information.

allies, Khmelnitsky at first won major victories which contributed to the downfall of the Kingdom of Poland but his allies deserted him and he fatally sought help from Muscovy, an Orthodox kingdom which was emerging as a significant power.

The alliance in 1654 brought immediate disappointment to the Cossacks. They had vowed allegiance to the Tsar and expected that his envoy, in the Tsar's name would vow allegiance to them. But no. And when Khmelnitsky presented the Tsar twenty pages of conditions, especially that the Tsar would respect Cossack independence and autonomy, the envoy replied that the Tsar respected nobody's conditions. So now the hopes of independence were dashed. Ukraine became known as Little Russia and has stayed like this in Russian minds until the present day. Russia honoured Khmelnytsky as a national hero who had brought Ukraine into 'the eternal union of all the Russias' (that is the Tsarist Empire which included large parts of Ukraine). So from now on, the Tsar decreed, Ukrainians would never break their ties with Great Mother Russia. The Soviets perpetuated the story and added that Khmelnytsky and his Cossacks had supported oppressed peasants against Polish landowners, which in fact they hadn't.

Yet the Cossacks kept their own traditions and although the tides of war and economic hardship saw many emigrate to Canada and elsewhere, they took with them their distinctive costume, their songs and folklore and the famous Cossack dance.

Their long, colourful history contains a dark side: cruel treatment of Ukraine's Jewish communities.

Their exotic dress and bravery attracted Romantic poets, writers and artists. They also feature in the stories of Isaac Babel, *Red Cavalry*, in which the author rides across Volyn with the Cossacks in the First Cavalry Army in 1920.

Lutsk

We leave Kremenets next day and set off to the bus station for Lutsk, the oldest town in Volyn, continuously lived in since the seventh century. It's about sixty miles from Kremenets, and approximately that same distance from the Polish border.

And that's why we've come. We're travelling here on behalf of an elderly Polish friend, Joseph Tarnowski who was taken from Lutsk under sentence of death when he was only eighteen. He survived to tell the tale, moved eventually to St Andrews and finally visited post-war Poland whose redrawn boundaries had cut him off from his home: it was too sad for him to travel the last sixty miles across the border to Ukrainian Lutsk.

We're also making this visit on behalf of Joe's school friend, Marian Feldman whose quick wits and map reading skills learnt in the Polish army cadets helped save him from the Holocaust. Marian and Joe met up in London long after the war – and met again through an exchange of memoirs as these two elderly men put their incredible stories into print (see pages 70-71).

The bus for Lutsk soon fills up. People stand in the aisle, a woman has an oversized wreath of plastic flowers. We're glad to get to our journey's end, although our immediate impression of Lutsk isn't the happiest one: Stalinist buildings and shops with cheap kitsch. We realise that this bleak vista is a sign of the ravages of war, the centre of Lutsk was heavily bombarded when the Red Army recaptured the town in 1944.

Indeed this historic town, like so many in Ukraine, has suffered the onslaught of too many armies all through its long history, not least in the twentieth century when, during the First World War alone, seven different armies fought one another in the town.

I'm reminded of a little girl in Warsaw who was asked, "Why do we study history?" She replied, "to find out who invaded us and why."

And if that's tragically true of Poland with its flat countryside and few natural boundaries, it is just oh so true of Ukraine.

But life goes on. We find a store which sells electrical goods. We haven't brought our small travelling kettle and Stuart who remembers his year in a student hostel in Leningrad, now St Petersburg, decides that we need an electric plunger, the sort you immerse into your cup to heat water or soup, which in my experience then cools very quickly.

LUTSK CASTLE

The language we speak has to be Russian. It doesn't matter in Kyiv, but here in Volyn people prefer Ukrainian. We always apologise and are graciously treated, but now a language problem brings confusion. Stuart bamboozles the ladies behind the counter by asking in Russian for a 'spiral'. I give him a nudge. He has just asked for a women's contraceptive, a coil! Once the ladies recover from their embarrassment and realise that we're foreigners, we all have a good laugh. We won't be able to brew a cup of tea, but we've booked into Hotel Ukraina and, fingers crossed, there may be a Western style room with a kettle, tea bags and coffee.

There isn't, but there's a wonderful restaurant. Waiting staff bring the meal to the table with military precision, lift the covers on the dishes in unison and place the plates on the table set with table linen that's almost too perfectly laundered to use.

We go into the Old Town; the Castle is the thing to see. It was built in the 13th century by Lithuanian princes on the site of a wooden fort built in the earliest years of the Rurik dynasty. The main tower of the Upper Castle, Lubart's Tower is such a symbol of Lutsk and of Volyn that it's featured everywhere, even on bank notes.

A custodian speaks to us. She has a wizened heart-shape face and a mass of ashen hair. She's interested in the old pagan Slavs. "History shows how our occupiers have treated us Ukrainians so badly. They always did us down – and it's still the same . . ." As she speaks she lowers her voice and looks nervously around.

"They took my grandfather to Siberia, he was well-off, you see, so they deported him. He worked felling trees. His arm got frost-bitten and had to be amputated. He survived and came home, there was an amnesty, but he had nowhere to go. Someone else had taken his home."

She shows us an unusual museum of bells. They come from Austria, France, Poland, Russia, there are church bells, a ship's bell, a bell for a train and even the bell that the postman rang when he brought the mail.

The museum of art is closed but she lets us look around just the same. It smells of damp, rising damp, of mice and neglect. There's a cat on the prowl 'because of the mice'. The paintings have mostly from the collection once owned by a great landowning family. The artists were Dutch, Spanish, French, Polish and Ukrainian, there was even a Scottish name, too faded to make out properly. We feel sad to see these paintings stacked together, not properly displayed and badly affected by the damp.

The restaurant, though, is the height of baronial elegance with every effort made to create the correct style with stag's heads, a boar's head and a set of antlers.

We chat to a young guy in the cloakroom. "The Communists ruined Ukraine," he says. "I'd like to see our language fully restored."

He points out the Polish cathedral, still being renovated. I remember how Joe Tarnowski had told us that he and his friends would rush into the Cathedral when the Host was raised so that they could tell their mothers that they had been to Mass.

We chat to a priest, Father Tomasz. He's from the south of Poland. He serves two parishes here, he has to dig walls and repair the fabric and wishes that the builders and electricians who have all flocked abroad to work would come back and help him.

The Cathedral has survived because it was turned into a museum of atheism.

"You obviously know how much easier church life is in Poland," the priest says. "My colleagues can't understand why I want to come here. When I first started there were just two old women, I thought it was worth it, just for two. People still look round in fear when they come into church and they're still scared to tell anyone that they've been. That's just how it is."

An elderly lady agrees. "We lived with fear, so scared that we'd be noticed. We had to come and pray in secret."

She tells us that her daughter is a lecturer in Polish language and her grand-daughter is studying journalism in Warsaw.

We say goodbye and head off for the large outdoor market beneath the Castle walls.

It's cold, zero degrees. I buy hand-knitted woollen socks and sheepskin gloves and feel much warmer. The gloves have cost the equivalent of £3.50 and last me for ages, in fact I lose them before they're fully worn out.

We visit a stall where a woman is selling her own embroidery. I buy a piece to take home as a present. A bystander gets into conversation. "What, you don't have family here? So who have you come to see?"

"You," Stuart tells her and she laughs – and laughs, as if it's the funniest thing ever.

"I was born in Poland," she says. "We got resettled here." And says no more. Her silence reminds us of the trauma of that so-called 'resettlement.'

The embroiderer, Masha is a Hutsul, an ethnic group with their own traditions and folklore who settled in the Carpathian Mountains centuries ago. She has come a long way and I'm glad to meet someone from such a different part of Ukraine, glad too to buy her work.

Warmed up, we explore the Old Town. The historic synagogue which dates from 1629 was the major synagogue in Jewish Lutsk. A guide book explains that it was originally erected on one condition – it must be well defended. The Jewish community was required to mount an armed guard; the main tower was built into the old city wall.

We were told that there were fifty synagogues and study houses in pre-war Lutsk. After the war the Communists used this building for a sports hall.

Karaite Street across the road is a reminder of the multi-cultural life of pre-war Lutsk. There were about seventy Karaite families in pre-war Lutsk who lived in small houses close beside their wooden *kenesa*, a picturesque building which dated back to the 18th century and hasn't survived. There are no Karaite adherents in Lutsk now, but Joseph Tarnowski tells us that two of his Karaite school friends survived the war. The Karaite faith is a branch of Judaism which acknowledges the Torah, the first five books of Moses. They still have a temple in Troki, Lithuania, which is only used in summer as it's unheated. They have a restaurant there too where we once enjoyed a meal beside a roaring fire. The owner gave Stuart a Karaite prayer book from 1937, we noticed that the Lord's Prayer was included, written in Polish.

Enough sight-seeing, it's time to return to Hotel Ukraina and get ourselves covered in mud from the Dead Sea, a new speciality offered by the hotel.

Our skilled masseuse with, she says, healing hands, pays special attention to Stuart's knee which is very swollen and becoming ever more painful. Clearly a knee replacement is on the horizon. Meantime, we rely on mud.

Our masseuse lives in a single room with her fourteen year old daughter and eight year old son. Her husband is in the police but neither earn enough to get credit to buy a bigger flat.

Well rested after this in-depth treatment, we go for a walk by the River Styr. It's said that the old name for Lutsk was *Luchersk*, called so because the town was founded on a bend in the river.

Young women tap by in smart knee high boots on highest heels. I just can't get over these boots. High fashion has clearly come to women's feet. Boots are red or blue or black, lacy, beribboned, the heels metallic, sharp as nails. They negotiate cobbled streets and badly set paving stones. Oh, those boots, each one is a work of art! Such a feature of new women in this new Ukraine!

We call at the Castle and visit a museum of the town. The custodian carefully lights each room and guides us through. Alas, it's dull, old-fashioned and propagandist. There's no attempt to give a picture of the old multi-ethnic Lutsk with its rich history. It's all presented as the Cossack struggle for freedom.

Delicate china, once the property of great landowning families, is crammed into display cases; priority is given to dusty farm implements and shoes of plaited birch bark once worn by farm workers. The First World War is mentioned – and then a jump to the Second, 'the Great Patriotic War' as the Soviets called it. Jewish life isn't represented, just information about the war-time ghetto. There's no mention of the era between 1921-39 when Lutsk belonged to the Polish Second Republic and was called Łuck. We write 'thank you' in the book but feel sad at such a miserable display and poor presentation.

Our walk by the river takes us past something that pulls us up sharp. Old gravestones which have obviously been torn up from some desecrated Polish cemetery are heaped crazily together on the river bank. Some names are still visible. The dates, as far as we can make out, are all 19th century, one is clearly marked as 1840.

Why are they here, we wonder, and when were they put here? What's the point of this heap of gravestones? Is it a kind of graffiti, a statement to denigrate well-to-do families who once lived in Lutsk?

On the other side of the path is a house like something out of a surreal fantasy. The house has a curved façade with an imposing a balcony on top. Some large windows are oval in shape, others are oblong and all

House with Chimeras [*photo @ ioannalexa www.dreamtimes.com*]

are crowned with elaborately carved stone or wood work – we're too far away to see – each one with its own design. The upper storey is surrounded with a balustrade, as though it had once been a roof garden. Tall white statues surmount these supports, with broken arches at the rear. It looks as if it had once been a beautiful villa, so much care has been taken into the design. Is it still lived in? And do the carvings in the walls that surround the house include gravestones? We wonder who created this bizarre set-up.

There's nobody to ask, and no plaque to indicate what it all means. Only much later, when we finally get back home I researched the house and discover that it's the brain child of an artist and sculptor, Mykola Holovan who built it on land given by the city authorities. The octogenarian artist has become a local phenomenon and his house is one of the go-to tourist attractions of Lutsk.

Just beyond this strange house the spire of a Gothic-style Protestant church points to the blue sky. It was once a Lutheran church and served the German community, a reminder of the multi-ethnic multi-faith culture of Lutsk, and indeed of all Volyn which had been annihilated by Nazi and Soviet ethnic cleansing. It's now a Baptist church. The typical pointed spire on the building reminds me that the Austrian poet Rainer Maria Rilke says in his *Stories of God* that Western church spires are like bayonets that threaten the heavens, while the round Orthodox domes sit gracefully and modestly in the landscape and threaten no-one.

Further along the bank we come across an orchard, red apples hang on the trees and people are picking the last of the crop. We're so used to seeing apples in supermarkets that it's a surprise and delight to see them glowing among the yellowing leaves of the trees.

Continuing our walk we pass some young lads drinking beer and a man who has stripped to the waist. He's thick-set and powerfully made, obviously proud of his bronze torso though perhaps not so proud of the grey hair curling over his chest.

There's a cold wind blowing but in spite of that a grey haired woman in an ill-fitting swimming costume is doing gymnastics on the bank after her swim.

"Was the water cold?"

"No, quite bearable. People swim here all the year round."

She's a maths teacher in a local secondary school. She makes the sign of the cross, wades back into the river and swims off with a gentle breast stroke, while two women who are totally unclad turn their backs to passers-by and stand behind a shed. A younger woman shakes her wet hair.

What a contrast to the spa we have just enjoyed, and to the women we saw in the hotel who were stunning, superbly dressed and made-up. These women are elemental, broad-shouldered and strong.

The sun lights up the old town, so beautiful, countrified with chickens clucking in gardens, apples showing red and green among the boughs and the first leaves falling. Beautiful Ukraine, where, in spite of bombardment and tyranny people still live close to the things that matter and, above all, know how to survive.

Another woman, who was strong in a different way, is remembered in a street name in Lutsk, Lesya Ukrainka Street. Her family had a house here. Larysa Petrovna Kosach was born in 1871 and became a leading writer in the Ukrainian language. Totally opposed to the Tsarist regime, she was taught at home so that she and her brother would be educated in Ukrainian. The siblings knew nine languages and later translated major works into Ukrainian.

Larysa started publishing her patriotic poetry in Ukrainian when she was very young and took the pen name Lesya (the forest girl) Ukrainka. The tsarist press didn't allow works in Ukrainian, the pen name was a cover for Larysa as well as a statement. Her novels, poems and plays were published in Galicia, the Habsburg controlled part of west Ukraine, where the censorship wasn't so strict, and were then smuggled into Kyiv.

Lesya developed bone TB, her family took her abroad to warmer countries. She died in a sanatorium in Tbilisi, Georgia aged only 42. There are statues dedicated to her in Ukraine and abroad, and as women's writing is now better known and acknowledged, Lesya is becoming an influencer in the new, independent Ukraine.

Two school friends and their different fates

Joe Tarnowski and Marian Feldman went to High School in Lutsk and both have written about their war time experiences, Joseph Tarnowski, with Raymond Raszkowski Ross, *Walking with Shadows*, Glen Murray Publishing, 2009 and Marian Feldman, *From Warsaw through Łuck, Siberia and back to Warsaw* translated Stuart Robertson, published Ryszard Feldman with lulu.com 2009.

When the Soviets invaded Lutsk in 1939 seventeen year old Joe joined the Polish Resistance was betrayed, tortured, put on trial and sentenced to death on Christmas Eve 1940. He was sent to the Gulag and, close to death, was saved when Hitler invaded the USSR and a Polish army was formed with the grudging consent of Stalin. Joe survived the war but never returned to Lutsk. His school friend, Marian Feldman had equally incredible adventures, many hardships and near death experiences. Marian did return to Lutsk, then in Soviet Ukraine where he found the street names had been changed, the house he had lived in had disappeared and, like us, years later, he was sad to see that there was no reference to the period between the wars, a formative part of his life had been wiped out.

Most Westerners only became fully aware about life in the USSR with the publication of Solzhenitsyn's books, especially his *Gulag Archipelago* in the 1970s. These two teenagers, Marian and Joe, along with so many other deportees, experienced Soviet life first hand and survived to tell the tale, though there were few in the West who wanted to hear or even believe, while in the Polish People's Republic, as in Ukraine, people had to get on with Moscow controlled reality and keep silent.

Stuart and I continue our quest to find the vanished world of Polish and Jewish culture, while absorbing the lovely land of golden wheat and flax, yellow sunflowers, sunshine and blue skies that is Ukraine. We want to visit more historic places and to research Kremenets and its famous Lyceum.

This quest took us to the archives which are stored in a large town called Ternopil in the lovely, though little visited, area called Podillya.

Chapter 3

Podillya

We fly Easy Jet to Kraków and then by inter-city express to the border town of Przemyśl where there's a long delay as train wheels are changed for the different gauge tracks and Ukrainian coaches are fastened on.

Ukrainian traders gather with huge bags. Is this stuff that they've not been able to sell in Poland? Or have they bought things to sell in Ukraine?

Our train conductor, grey haired and with a Lech Wałęsa moustache equips us with laundered sheets, bottled water, towels, and soap. It's good to stretch out after our early start from Edinburgh. We will have a short night, though, the train will get into Ternopil at 2.30 am.

Our conductor wakens us. He's been doing this journey for thirty years. In the old Communist days, he says, guards patrolled the train corridors with guns and big dogs, while in the Solidarity days they had tanks at the border. "The Soviets were just biding their time, waiting for the chance to cross into Poland and spill Polish blood once again. That's how it was, that was the way of it."

He helps us down with our cases. "Haven't you got anyone meeting you? Well, have a good stay."

He disappears into the night.

Ternopil

The town on the shores of the lake is relatively modern compared with many others we've visited in Ukraine. It was founded in the 16th century.

The great attraction is a large lake with two hotels on opposite sides, both very Soviet in appearance. We have been given a renovated room which overlooks a restored church. We ask if we could have a lakeside view. "Of course you can," says our friendly receptionist, "but that side hasn't been modernised yet." She opens a room door to let us see and we immediately agree that, attractive though the view is, comfort is more important and we accept the room she has given us.

So, having rested after our broken night, we head for the lake where a man is fishing from the promenade beside the grey water. It's cold, ten degrees and everyone is wrapped up warmly. Toddlers chase pigeons or walk sedately hand in hand with Mum who wears the inevitable high-heeled boots and carries a large bunch of autumn leaves to bring nature into her apartment.

You can buy everything right at the roadside from the latest smart phones and lap tops to garlic, onions, plums, grapes and lots more. A plump woman in a booth sells buns filled with sausage and cabbage. Oh, the good smell, this chilly day and the warmth spreading through us as we share the delicacy straight from pots full of sizzling fat!

An elderly woman is selling embroidery, the pieces are pegged out on a rope behind her. She wears an ankle length grey coat and a rust-red beret. Her eyes behind her large glasses with white plastic frames are gentle and friendly. "My mother used to sew and I decided to take it up when I became a pensioner."

"Yes," I say, "my sister does embroidery too."

"Are you visiting your sister?"

I realise she can't quite understand why we would come to Ternopil without having family to visit. I buy a piece of her work for my sister.

It's time to visit the archives housed in a large church, once a Roman Catholic convent, Greek Catholic now. We walk across a worn carpet over a bumpy floor. Are any nuns buried underneath, I wonder, remembering Dubno and Nikolay the icon painter. We make ourselves known to a receptionist. The head of the archives, Bohdan, keeps us waiting on wooden chairs in a corridor which is hung with stark black and white photographs of the *Holodomor*, the terrible famine which resulted in the deaths of millions. It was inflicted by Stalin and his henchmen in 1932-33 to force peasant farmers to accept collectivisation.

We finally get permission to enter an old fashioned room with rows of desks where a bored young woman invigilates. Photocopying is expensive and no cameras are allowed on pain of being brought before Director Bohdan and chucked out of the archives.

During our time in the archives, one poor delinquent reader gives a wee fly click of a camera and great are the ructions thereat. The bored girl springs into action, the director is summoned, no excuses are accepted and we look at an empty desk for the rest of the afternoon.

I can't say that our research has borne much fruit. We're not too sure what we're looking for or what context to put it in, but I have learnt something of the enlightened education at the Polish Lyceum between the wars as well as the repression of a movement *Prosvita* which undertook Ukrainian teaching in village schools.

The archives will be closed tomorrow, so we'll explore Podillya. The fertile countryside is cut through by great rivers, crowned with forests and has more than its fair share of ruined castles and mighty forts. I recalled the story of the Greek girl, the rags to riches Countess Sofia who became first Lady of the Castle at Kamianets and the surrounding area. With the help of our excellent guide book which has already taken us round Volyn we have earmarked two towns to visit: Buchach and Berezhany.

We wake up to a beautiful day. The sun is warm, even hot behind glass, the promised *babino lito* ('old woman's summer' or Indian summer) is on the way.

At breakfast we enjoy fried eggs, which taste so very fresh, bacon, tomatoes, cheese and bread, but only one cup of hot water with the dreaded tea bag placed at the side along with two sugar lumps. I don't like tea bags but never mind, out we go. The lake water is sparkling in the sun and fishermen are already at work. Two young guys stand in a small bay to cast their rods, while elderly gents sit on folding chairs, obviously prepared for a long wait, doubtless fuelled by vodka.

Bus ride from Ternopil to Buchach

Buses pull in and out of the busy terminus. Here's one for Lviv, a three hour journey away. Our bus will leave at 9.30, a one and a half hour journey to cover 60 kilometres. We notice a blue building marked in large white letters TYALET. From the look of the outside it wouldn't win the toilet of the year award and with memories of other bus station toilets on our travels we're glad we're not on a long distance journey.

The bus fills up quickly. Women stand. A girl is forced to stand uncomfortably on the bottom step. Everyone holds heavy bags, no one puts their luggage on the floor. Are they scared it will get snatched, I wonder.

We cruise along in the middle of the road to the strains of Abba, *It's a rich man's world* . . . O, irony! We come to a bus stop. No, there's no more room, but the driver stops and a woman in a roll neck sweater and leather jacket gets on with a teenage boy. They push into the crowd and stand patiently.

We're the only tourists, the only people travelling for pleasure.

The countryside of Podillya stretches ahead of us. There are strips of ploughed soil with no sign of human habitation, just marks of a tractor turning the good, dark soil. The road seems as rutted as the ploughed-up earth.

Now woods stretch out on either side of the road. Cars are parked on the verge. Mushroom pickers are already hard at work in the forest. A Ukrainian Saturday outing.

The bus struggles up a steep hill. Maize grows in stiff rows. A large house takes pride of place on the crown of the hill. Its owners have probably worked abroad and built the house with the money they saved. The driver stops and leaves the bus, he takes the key with him. Music thumps on meaninglessly and women stand burdened and patient.

The driver returns; three chickens scatter as the bus negotiates a bend. We pass a new church, gold glistens as gold as the teeth in people's mouths.

We cross the River Seret. There are two graveyards to the right and left of us. One is well tended with bright flowers, flags and statues of heroes. The other is neglected, abandoned. Who now remembers the forsaken dead?

More woods. More parked cars.

Stooks of hay are neatly tied. Pumpkins lie like golden footballs all over the fields. An old man tends three cows. An old woman is bowed to the ground with a lumpy sack on her back. A man sells water melons from the back of a truck and women queue to buy.

One passenger gets off our crowded bus, the girl who stands on the step still clutches her plastic bags. She has to get out to let people in or out.

Two cows are followed by a third with a calf chained to her. A wayside cross is drowned in flowers.

The bus stops. We've arrived and everyone gets off.

Buchach

We walk up the steep road, it's paved but dusty. The autumn weather is very warm. We glimpse a ruined castle, spires and roof tops half hidden by trees and come to a small church. We want to look inside, but the main door is locked. A mother comes in with two small children to look at the pictures in the foyer: Jesus blesses barefoot children in national dress.

Outside the church a large wooden cross rises on a hilltop. It's garlanded with blue and yellow flowers and is a memorial to the Ukrainian nationalists, murdered in the crypt of this church. Further into the town centre the grandiose Baroque Town Hall, a UNESCO heritage site, is covered in scaffolding. It stands alone in its own square and is truly magnificent with its ornamented façade and a tower soaring high. It was built by the powerful Pototsky family whom Sofia married into; their coat of arms pops up everywhere in Buchach. The Town Square is deserted. Church bells are ringing. It's noon. We notice a small museum. I ask the young man at the desk if he has any postcards for sale. There are none, he says. His name is Mykola. He can speak Polish and Russian but prefers Ukrainian. He works as a history teacher and tour guide and shows us round the museum with richly embroidered, folk costumes on display. "These costumes are typically Polish," Mykola explains, "and these garments over here were made by Lemkov people," and adds, "they were evicted from their villages in Poland."

I recall a forsaken wooden church we had once seen in the hills of southern Poland. It had belonged to the displaced Lemkov community, there was nobody left to pray there because of the brutality and total injustice of Operation Vistula. Politicians draw lines on maps and the human suffering this entails is appalling. Each side has its murderers who carried out their task with utter depravity. And each side has its victims.

It's good to see Polish and Lemkov folk art displayed together in this small Ukrainian museum which also celebrates famous people from Buchach, including a Nobel Prize winner, the Hebrew writer Samuel Agnon.

Mykola points out historic postcards from the Austrian Empire and large banknotes, both Austrian and Russian. He tells us of work by an Austrian born artist whose sculptures are in a local church. He had worked in local stone from a nearby town called Yasloviets, as well as in sandstone brought from 200 miles away. "Haven't you got a car, oh that's a pity I could have shown you Yasloviets. It's so beautiful. And the countryside is lovely too . . . Let me show you Buchach. I love my town."

Yes, Yasloviets . . . a regiment of that name distinguished itself in 1944 at the Battle of Monte Cassino.

As we go through empty streets Mykola explained that the town is deserted because it's the festival of the Finding of the True Cross. Everyone's in church – more than two thousand people attend the solemn service.

He shows us a plaque on the side of a nicely painted house. It commemorates the writer Agnon who had lived in Buchach before he emigrated to Israel. Simon Wiesenthal, later known as a hunter of Nazi war criminals, also lived here until he endured imprisonment in five different concentration camps, the last one was Mauthausen.

Wiesenthal was a big man in every sense. Even in his nineties he filled his modest office in Vienna. The shelves were full of brown paper files and documents, all crammed together, all charting the Holocaust and Wiesenthal's commitment to justice. I met him when I went to Vienna with a Polish-Jewish group from Warsaw. Wiesenthal was an unforgettable figure.

Emanuel Ringelblum was another prominent citizen of Jewish Buchach. Incarcerated in the Warsaw ghetto, Ringelblum was the instigator and chief archivist of a remarkable collection of letters, diaries and documents that chart the Holocaust even as it was happening. After the Ghetto Uprising in May 1943, Ringelblum was rescued from a concentration camp and went into hiding along with his wife, teenage son and thirteen other people. The hiding place was betrayed and everyone was executed, along with the Polish man of the house and his fifteen year old son.[1]

Now we turn right up fairly steep road and come to a well. The faded inscription says that Jan Sobieski, King of Poland and Grand Duke of Lithuania had drunk from this well. Aha, Scottish links here. Bonnie Prince Charlie's mother was Clementina Sobieska.

"I know this Scottish history," Mykola says and we continue our tour.

The houses here are much better kept than the ones in Kremenets had been. Flowers in pots and boxes cascade over wrought iron balconies. These houses were built by the Austrians, Mykola says and had also belonged to Jewish families, and so were those over there – and he points to cottage style houses with overgrown gardens gone to seed.

We turn another steep corner and now we have a good view of the town. The church service is still in progress. We can hear the choir singing their beautiful liturgy. The space in front of the magnificent Baroque church is black with people who haven't been able to fit into the packed building. The road is lined with dozens of parked cars.

Passers-by greet Mykola, "*Slava Isusu*," Glory to Jesus. He replies, "*Slava na viky*." Glory for ever.

"Did people use this greeting in the Communist era?" we ask. "Yes, in the country they did. Communists just said 'good day.'"

Mykola tells us that his father, who is now sixty-eight, had been deported here from south east Poland. The journey had taken a month in a cattle wagon. They had to leave everything behind. His father always says, "We live well now, but it was poverty then."

We notice building work going on. Mykola tells us that tourists say, "So many big houses and such poor roads." That's because these houses

---

1   From Samuel D. Kassow, *Who will write our history?* Penguin Books, London 2007, 385.

are private, says Mykola, we build them ourselves. The roads – well that's the government or town council. "My friends go to England or to Portugal and Spain to work, I've got ten friends there just now. Yes, illegal and legal. Then they come back and build these big houses."

He shows us the local Polish Catholic church. Father Rutyna the priest had led his sorrowing Polish congregation away from the town in 1945 when the Communists took over; as soon as freedom came the elderly priest returned and won everyone's admiration when he rolled up his sleeves, hitched up his cassock and got busy with rebuilding the church. Now in his nineties, he's become a legend like Irena in Kremenets. He's is in Poland just now – he hasn't been so well.

A tour bus arrives as we return to the Town Hall, the most beautiful in all Ukraine, Mykola says. Two people approach Mykola and ask about the church. Of course for these Polish tourists that means the Roman Catholic one. Each group has its own interest points.

And for Poles, the list is long. And for Jews, well, there's the house of the Nobel prize-winning author Samuel Agnon. And, alas, alas, the dead. The Jewish cemetery to which Mykola is now taking us.

The historic gravestones crowd close together and reach right to the roadside. Sigmund Freud's grandparents are buried here. The family later moved to Vienna whence Freud's elderly sisters had been transported to be murdered in Treblinka.

Mykola leads us along steep paths through the graveyard to a memorial stone whose fading lettering in English records the murder of 15,000 Jewish people who had been shot in mass executions in the valley. From this memorial stone we look across the valley. Houses rise amidst the trees. Did people hear the shooting, the cries?

More woodland has grown up since. It was Soviet policy, says Mykola; and we recall that so many Soviet memorials mark the martyrdom of patriots and don't ever mention that many if not all of the dead were Jewish.

Mykola shows us an eating place. The place he indicates isn't grand or prepossessing but the food is excellent. At the next table sits Granny, broad of beam, along with two sisters with a child apiece and an old lady who's obviously a guest of honour.

A post-prandial stretch out would be lovely and eventually we find a grassy spot beside the ruined Buchach castle. Those stout stone walls and thick archways had driven back Tatars and Turks and many other invading armies and now provide a nice enclosed place for us to have a wee snooze in the kindly sun.

The Town Hall clock pings and chimes.

We retrace our steps down a steep track between cottages with neat gardens, geraniums grow in pots beside whitewashed walls. A tethered goat grazes contentedly on a sheer slope with well nibbled grass. As we replenish our water bottle back at the well where King Jan Sobieski once drank, a voice hails us, "Stuart!" And there is the ever friendly Mykola. He had no lunch, just a sandwich, conducted a Polish tour group and now here he is again, eager to be of help.

We visit the huge church we had seen earlier, empty now of all the worshippers. It had been Polish once and the iconostasis sits uncomfortably amongst Baroque splendour. Outside are the forbidding walls of what had once been a large monastery. It had been a prison under the Soviets. About a dozen monks live there now, and it's a boys' boarding school, very patriotic and religious, says Mykola. There are boys here from Serbia and Romania; we catch up with two of them on our walk, one wears a white shirt with a black band around the collar, the other wears a traditional Ukrainian embroidered shirt, all in honour of the Festival.

Mykola shows us an ornate Art Nouveau house that an Italian family had built as a private residence. Tsarist armies who occupied Buchach in the First World War turned it into a military hospital.

A family came here recently all the way from Austria, Mykola says. Their Jewish grandmother had been a doctor in this First World War hospital and had shown the family photographs of the building, they had come all the way here to see it.

It's time to head down for the bus. As we pass the museum Mykola brings his boss out to meet us and we say a last goodbye.

"I wanted you to have a good time in Buchach," Mykola says. "It's been so interesting," we assure him.

And indeed as we stand at the bus stop and look back at the way the town seems to grow organically among the trees, I think that Buchach is my favourite place so far in our exploration.

Bus ride back to Ternopil

Two young teenage girls wait for the bus. They're going to a 'house of culture' where they learn folk dancing.

On board a woman with a bouffant hair style and lots of luggage speaks in a foreign language on her phone. "Magyar?" Stuart asks, and they launch into an animated conversation. She's Ukrainian from Mukachevo, a town that had been Hungarian before the Second World War.

Black and white photographs from the album, *Vanished World* with scenes of pre-war Jewish Mukachevo spring to my mind.

That was then, and should not be forgotten. An elderly scholar in Poland wrote an article on the eve of Poland's joining the EU, *To Europe, yes, but together with our dead*. The countries of the former Eastern bloc need to reclaim their history's dark pages as well as its bright heroics. Not for nothing did Joe Tarnowski call his memoir, *Walking with Shadows*. I don't apologise for introducing shadows as well as light to my exploration of Ukraine.

Anyway, here I am at the back of the jolting bus sitting beside a very young boy, perhaps ten or eleven. His hair is cropped close to the scalp, almost shaven, he wears military uniform. "Excuse me, are you a junior cadet?" I ask in Russian. "I'm in the military lyceum in Ternopil," he replies.

So young and all alone! I'd like to ask a bit more about his life and studies but I don't know how much Russian he knows and I don't want to embarrass him. I wonder where he is now, in 2023, in what embattled region of Ukraine he serves.

I watch the sun slant across the hillsides and quiet farm land. Clear skies promise more good weather. We pass a neat village green, a small town with shops, as well as houses with satellite dishes. Two women chat, they carry empty buckets, and now we pass another deserted graveyard, cows graze among the graves.

And now we've arrived and the lake water is still and mirror-like reflects the quiet sky. We eat dinner at a restaurant by the lake. It's warm enough to sit outside where we watch the young cool people of Ternopil parade along the promenade outside our hotel.

Berezhany – and a hidden pearl

We decide to explore picturesque Berezhany, about fifty kilometres away.

We leave our hotel room, press the button for the lift to go down and find that the whole space is taken up by a big, big military man, whose high hat and corpulence designate his importance. He's carrying a bulging suitcase and a suit in a protective cover. We squeeze into the lift. The man only grunts when Stuart says hello. His heavy breathing gets worse as he struggles along the corridor. Luckily a car is waiting for him.

We leave the hotel. Mist lies across the lake. The sun as pale as the moon, leaves a widening stream of silver across the molten water.

It's back to the Ternopil bus station for us. We've come early enough to sit in the front, before the bus fills up and bag after bag gets piled on.

The bus station in Berezhany is quiet and clean. Stuart helps a girl carry her bag off the bus. It's so heavy that he can hardly lift it. She takes it back, she already has a huge bag in the other hand, and along with other laden passengers she heads to the other side of the bus station for her onward journey to a village somewhere.

And now the town is ours to explore.

"Castle first," Stuart insists.

Its mighty walls tower above the river. Apparently it withstood even the Cossack invasions but aristocratic owners with too many castles let it fall into disrepair, while all the wars and invasions of the twentieth century added to its sad decline. It was once magnificent, a great example, our guide book says, of a Renaissance fortified residence, it's a sad ghost now. Headless effigies and crumbled carvings are poor relics of the glories of the past. A church, once a private chapel, is being restored.

Outside the ruin we chat to three cyclists. They've come from Lviv and will return this evening, a round trip of a hundred and sixty-eight kilometres.

"That's nothing," says the man who sells tickets for a castle visit. "We've had a couple here from Switzerland. They cycled the whole way."

And so to the town. Our guide book calls Berezhany the pearl of Podillya, both from the point of view of its location and its many historic buildings. There's almost no traffic. It seems like a stage set that's waiting for the action to take place. There's a historic Town Hall and a large square graced by a beautiful Greek Catholic church. Everything is clean and tidy, and although it's almost noon nobody seems astir. Coffee calls. We go into what seems a community centre where tables are set for a feast.

"There's to be a christening," the smiling waitress tells us. "Come and join the party. You'll be very welcome." She makes us a toasted ham and cheese sandwich to go with the coffee.

Following our guide book we find the Armenian church with only a plaque to say what it once was. The Armenians left in 1945 and the church remains redundant with the attractive parish house next door still unoccupied. Then comes the Polish parish church. It towers over the square, a great example, we read, of Gothic-Renaissance architecture but now in need of plaster and paint. It survived so many wars only to be used first as a grain store and then as a sports hall by the Communists.

There's a service in progress. We stand at the back. We've arrived at just the right moment, the christening is taking place and the baby is being named, however our attention is diverted to a plaque which informs us that Rydz-Śmigly, Commander in Chief of the Polish Armed forces before the Second World War was baptised in this church.

Outside in the courtyard a couple are kissing deeply, we tactfully back away, though they're too involved to notice us.

Back on the square we enter the former Polish grammar school, which young Rydz once attended. It now houses three museums; we get a warm welcome in the House of Books. A row of black and white photographs of Ukrainian writers covers one wall. Two ladies offer tea and biscuits. Life is hard, the women say. They have to take holidays without pay. We survive, they say, because we're optimists.

They tell us about the part writers played in encouraging Ukrainian independence through their books.

I feel ashamed that I know absolutely nothing about Ukrainian literature. I know about the national poet Taras Shevchenko, you can't miss, him, every town has a street called after him. And Gogol, though he wrote in Russian, and Lesya Ukrainka, but that's it. However I wish that House of Books would also display Polish and Jewish writers who once lived and studied here.

As I look at the large town square and the well preserved houses that surround it, I imagine it how it was when the Austrians were in charge. It seems so little changed that I can almost hear the strains of the Radetsky March and imagine officers on horseback who trot ceremoniously through the town and show off their gaudy epaulettes, jewelled sword hilts and spurs.

We wander on in search of a seventeenth century Orthodox church, made entirely of wood. Instead, we come across an enormous brick building under construction. I stop to take a photo. "*Pani* (madam)," an old man says, "what do you think of this monstrosity? Make sure you show them back home this church with its squint dome." He's little with white hair and white teeth, with half missing. "Let them see what rubbish builders the Russkies are," he says, or words to that effect.

We find the old wooden church a kilometre further on, and, oh dear, it's shut, but two women and a man are sitting in the foyer. "Did you see that hideous church they're building?" one of the women says. "The church council made us do it," her friend adds. "We haven't got the money to build such a thing. The Catholics get money from Poland, the Greek Catholics have heaps of cash, nobody helps us. Our priest is marvellous, though, simply from heaven. You can really talk to him. Yes, there are lots of Catholics, but hardly any Poles. He . . ." she nudges the man beside her, "'he was from Poland. He was re-settled here. I was only two, but I've heard the stories." She wipes her eyes. "No, I wasn't resettled myself, I just feel so sorry for those who were."

This little group say they have over a hundred parishioners, they all have to give money for the new grandiose church. They think, and I agree, that they'd be much better to stay in their centuries old wooden church whose planks were fitted together without nails or screws.

Lunch next in a small café. I have dumplings. I hoped they'd come filled with mushrooms, but there are none, they're filled with potato instead. Stuart has schnitzel with chips and we both have cabbage salad. More guests come in. I wonder why they're not at home enjoying a hearty Ukrainian Sunday lunch. We chat for a bit, pay our bill and go out into the sunshine.

And now so unexpectedly, we stumble upon a hidden pearl. It's a ruin, but still imposing. The outside walls show how well built it was, there's even some glass in two small triangular windows. A metal Star of David frames another glassless window. More round windows and arches given an impression of something so important, so treasured for centuries until . . .

The ground floor has its own story to tell. It's below street level, so only when you step down can you see the height and majesty of the building, not visible from street level. A synagogue must never be more prominent than a church, so deep foundations had to be built and you enter the heights of religion by going down. "Out of the depths have I cried to thee, O Lord."[2]

Three main walls survive, one leans dangerously outwards. The roof has partially collapsed, but still holds its precarious own. Great sheets of metal swing eerily. Beams piled in a corner bear the marks of burning. I detect what could be Hebrew lettering on one wall, but it's too faint to make it out. One window frame is still intact, its wood blackened by fire but still unbroken.

Outside a rusty plaque says, 'a historical building, 16th century.' No mention that this was a meeting place for prayer and worship for the Jewish community, some of whom lived in the houses that cluster around their synagogue. And, I later learn that the date is wrong, the building was founded in the seventeenth century.

---

2   Psalm 130 KJV.

Old Synagogue at Berezhany

As we stand in the synagogue we hear bells ring from the Holy Trinity Church in the central square. Singing resounds from a loud speaker. An evening service has begun.

It's time to go back to the bus stop. I'm reluctant to leave this place of memory. I stoop and pick up a small tile, just two inches square. It sits on my bookcase at home.

On the bus we chat to a mother with a little boy from an outlying village. The wee boy is four and can count up to ten in English. His father works in Portugal, his mother goes to visit him from time to time and leaves her son with his grandparents, "The money's not that good," she says. "We're trying to work out whether to move to Portugal or just stay here."

The bus fills up. Young people are returning to Ternopil after a weekend at home.

Back in the archive we're told that two journalists want to interview us for a local paper. One man, a professor with the inevitable gold teeth wants to practise his hesitant English, he buttonholes me, rather than Stuart. This man was in England ten years ago, in Bradford, there's a large Ukrainian community there, he says, even a Saturday school. He says he taught in a primary school. The pupils were mainly non-English speaking, and I can't help wondering how they'd understood one another. I get the impression it wasn't a happy experience for him.

He says he's been to Poland lots of times. His wife's parents live there. They're Lemkovs, he says, who had been 'resettled.'

"That was a dreadful time, hard, cruel. A terrible time."

Next day when the paper comes out, although they'd interviewed both of us, it's only about Stuart. This is still a patriarchal society. Women don't count.

The lady in the newspaper kiosk knows who we are. "I read all about you in the paper," she tells us.

Our time in Ternopil has come an end. We pack, ready for a 3.30 am departure. Stuart tries to book a taxi but the telephone line is bad and he's not at all sure that the booking has gone through.

Indeed when he phones next morning we realise that there had been no previous booking. "A car will come in fifteen minutes," a voice assures him.

Here's hoping! We lug our cases to reception where the weary girl takes our key. I'm under the happy delusion that we can wait in a nice armchair in reception in the warm hotel, but no, we have to go out to the taxi stand.

Car headlights appear, none for us.

"She wouldn't let us wait in the hotel because she wants to have a lie down," Stuart says.

Yes, guests arrive all through the night, and we've inconvenienced her with our early departure.

The taxi arrives. At the station no one can tell us which platform we'll find the train on.

The large waiting room is a little slice of hell. Abject humanity is slumped on hard chairs, peasant women with burdens wait for what, why and to where? The air is foetid. The world is weary. A poor demented soul walks around. She talks endlessly to herself. She wears a ragged coat, long coloured socks, dirty trainers, a big, cowboy style hat. She's in a world of her own, but who threw her out, who cares for her, what will become of her?

The train comes in, we escape so much human misery, climb up the high metal steps and stretch out in our bunks. Night journeys are the way people still travel across great tracts of land here in Ukraine. They haven't modernised the roads – and no Beeching foolishly tore up the railway lines. A sleeper service saves time, hotel fees and is far more environmentally friendly than road and air travel.

And now here we are back in Kyiv where Stuart has been asked to take services at the Anglican church once again. I'm invited to give a talk in the British Council to English speaking Ukrainians. I wax lyrical about Volyn and Podillya and my audience is amazed. "These are backward and primitive places, we never think of going there. But maybe we should get to know our own country a bit better," they agree.

Yes, indeed, but that will only be possible when Ukraine is free of ruthless bombardment and devastating missile attacks.

Chapter 4

Bears

Bears and a child's plastic shoe

A truck drives into a clearing deep in a forest. There's a ticking sound as the engine dies, then silence, just birdsong and the wind in the trees. Masha raises her head. She smells the forest, scents out small furry creatures, feels a shaft of sunlight across her matted fur. She would like to go out and explore. This is her birthright, her world, this is where she belongs. But that was before the cage, the blows and threats, the sticks, the dogs. Now Masha is too scared to move.

The men who make money out of her force her outside. A hand tugs her iron collar. This collar is too tight, it cuts her neck, there are worse cuts to come. The men drag her to a tree. She turns her head. Trees are there to be climbed, to scratch a furry body and sharpen teeth against rough bark. Masha does none of these things. She's chained against the tree. The chain is tight. She chokes. She can't move.

And now the dogs are let loose. The torment begins and she can't defend herself. She makes a lunge with one paw – at least they haven't cut her claws. There's no need, she's too tightly tied. The dogs are excited, the men cheer them on and pass the vodka around. The attacks begin in earnest.

It's illegal but this deep in the forest there's nobody around to hear the frenzied barking, the baying of the hunting dogs, the sad moans of the bear.

It's over, they push Masha back into the truck. Blood soaks her brown fur. She's driven back to a run-down farmstead. There's a cage inside a barn. They lock her in.

Oh, Masha! She's ten years old and this is all she knows – until workers from a rescue charity turn up. There are threats and denials. "She's our family pet. Our kids love her. This deep cut in her neck, this open sore, well, that's just because her collar's a bit too tight. We keep meaning to get her a new one. So just get out, will you. This is private property. This is our bear."

"The police have been informed. They'll be here any moment."

They give way and Masha is carried away to begin a new life as the first bear in the Nadiya Bear Rescue centre, sponsored by Four Paws, an Austrian charity.

Bears have been my thing since 2008 when Stuart and I last left Ukraine. We went home via Warsaw where we chanced upon an exhibition of photographs of aspects of the Second World War which could be spoken about only in whispers in Communist Poland. And there I saw a picture of a Syrian brown bear called Wojtek (pronounced Voy-tek). Born in the mountains of Iran in 1942, the orphan cub was adopted by Polish soldiers and, a true war hero, carried live ammunition for the men of the Transport Corps at the Battle of Monte Cassino. At the end of the war the bear went into exile with the soldiers and ended his days in Edinburgh Zoo.

I wrote his story for older primary school children. *Wojtek, War Hero Bear* (Birlinn, Edinburgh) was published in 2014, the year a beautiful monument to Wojtek and to the Polish soldiers was unveiled in Prince Street Gardens with marvellous ceremony and atrocious weather. And now I want to find out more about bears, so I'm delighted to find the web site for a charity called Four Paws who rescue abused wild animals, including bears; they have a centre near Zhitomir, in Ukraine.

We fly to Kyiv where the wild life researcher for Four Paws meets us with her husband. I'd been imagining a plump middle aged, Soviet academic, and here is this highly qualified young woman. Maryna has studied, and written about the flora and fauna of the Carpathians including bears and lynx. She gives us her book, packed full of information. Her photograph is on the back cover along with her pet, a huge husky dog, or is it a German shepherd, or can it even be . . . yes, a wolf. Little and slim, she's dwarfed by him as she presses her cheek against his fur.

"I got him when he was young and brought him up just like a dog," she says. "It's not something I recommend. In fact I don't know anyone else who could do it safely, but it works for me."

Her husband lives dangerously too. He's a biologist and conservationist and makes frequent field trips to the Chernobyl area. He says it's safe, there's no radiation where he goes, it's incredible how nature renews itself, plants proliferate and vegetation flourishes.

We go to a café near the airport and Maryna tells us more about the Nadiya Bear Rescue centre – Nadiya means hope. It's in a village called Berezivka, near Zhitomir. We'll go there by bus, just about two hours from the bus station in Kyiv. Sasha who's in charge of the centre will meet us and tell us all we want to know.

It's getting dark when we arrive, Sasha is locking up. He has booked us into Hotel Ukraina in Zhitomir and drives us there.

We pass a granite rock at the entrance to the town which proclaims, Zhitomir 800. *Zhito* means rye and *mir* means peace, a nice pastoral image, but since its foundation in the year 800 Zhitomir, like the other cities and towns we've visited, has experienced more than its fair share of war and destruction, including during the present Russian invasion when schools and hospitals suffered missile attacks.

Hotel Ukraina is nice and central. It doesn't quite match up to the Hotel Ukraina in Lutsk where we enjoyed de-luxe comfort, excellent meals and a massage in Dead Sea mud; here we're back in the old Soviet style. The twin beds are lumpy. I put an extra blanket under the sheet and ignore the rather fusty smell.

Never mind, five nights' bed and breakfast here costs £50 for us both, so we're not complaining.

After breakfast we're happy to have a lift to the Nadiya Rescue Centre. A wooden brown bear, giant size and fierce-looking, welcomes us at the entrance along with a board with photographs of the five bears currently in the centre. The information about each bear is written in Ukrainian and English. Each bear has its own name with photographs of it before and after the arrival at the centre.

Sasha shows round a lecture hall with posters and information about bears and other wildlife in the Carpathian Mountains. Films are shown here with discussions on conservation. School children come in groups, others visit with their families for day out. A paved path runs right round the large enclosure where the bears are kept behind extra strong wire fencing, dug deep into the ground so it can't be pushed over, the bears can't escape and thieves can't break in and injure or steal the bears.

Within this enclosure each bear has its own sizeable patch of ground, fenced off from the other bears. A mound of stones has been constructed in each area, high enough to climb on and hollowed out to become a den for hibernation or shelter. When Masha came to the centre she had no idea how to hibernate, none of them had, but they've learnt now.

Each bear has its own fresh water swimming pool with a waterfall; trees with overhanging branches to climb or swing on, strong wooden ladders like an outsize climbing frame, upturned logs to balance on, an old tyre acts as a swing.

Masha lives in the middle area of this ursine estate. The sunshine of early April shines on her glossy coat. She rolls on her back, four paws in the air, a good advert for the charity, and balances delicately on a log, for all the world like a circus bear.

MASHA WITH TYRE

Which she isn't, though her two neighbours, Julia and Zoya, both siblings, had been forced to work in a circus. Not surprisingly, Julia hates being stared at. She prefers to swim in her pool for hours, often submerged, or hides in her cave. She and Zoya had been kept in separate cages, side by side for ten years, unable to have any contact with one another. The cages with a bare concrete floor were so cramped that the bears couldn't turn around. They never went outside, except to perform. In spite of a long tradition of performing bears, these animals are not naturally responsive to music. A friend sent me a piece on how dancing bears were trained. Their hind paws were swathed in rags. They were led into a room with a heated floor which forced them to raise their unprotected forepaws and stand upright. Many who failed to perform were mutilated. Zoya's trainer blinded her when he flung acid in her eyes. She had her teeth pulled and her jaw broken. She wanders like a poor shadow through her enclosure.

The other two bears in the Nadiya centre are much younger. Bodiya, the only male in the group was spotted by people from a television company who bought him from his owner, a man with more money than compassion, who had kept the young cub on display. He hasn't endured cruel torture but he'll never be able to fend for himself in the wild, and nor will Nastya the other younger bear who was found in a private zoo which had no proper facilities for its animals.

Each bear receives regular check-ups from a vet and there might even be attempts to mend Zoya's broken jaws.

Sasha takes us into the building where the vet works. This wooden building behind the wire fencing is entered by raised trap doors from each bear's own separate enclosure. The doors are then shut while treatment is carried out. The same system operates at feeding time. Each bear vacates its enclosure while Sasha puts fruit and vegetables in nooks and crannies for the bears to find, so there's an element of hunting, they're not spoon fed, except for Zoya who is given a bowl of specially made porridge.

Sasha tells us that when the vet is satisfied with the health and progress of each bear they will be moved to a large sanctuary outside Lviv, where they will live in a semi-wild but still protected state.

We often wonder now, in 2023, what has happened to these bears and their sanctuary in this war, as pitiless for animals as it is for humans.

Outside the Bear Centre we discover a small café with its own kitchen. We enjoy a plate of excellent borsht, steaming hot from the stove. No microwaves here!

Borscht

We talk about bears. Bear baiting was once a popular entertainment, especially in Shakespeare's London. I quote the reference to bear baiting in *Macbeth*:

They have tied me to a stake; I cannot fly,

But bear-like I must fight the course . . .

Masha's injuries were horrific and so was the life she led as a baited bear, not for public entertainment but to train hunting dogs; both ways are abhorrent and so is the use of animals in circuses. We wonder if bears of all animals are particularly subject to abuse and not just in Europe; in Asia they are literally – and illegally – milked for their bile for use in Chinese medicine, while the British Army still insists on bearskin helmets, though these come from culled black bears in Canada.

Well, the little shop beside the café doesn't sell bearskin, thank goodness, though I have my eye on traditional sheepskins. Stuart enjoys acute hearing but he's totally deaf when it comes to shopping, unless it's for books. So my request to look at the sheepskin passes by unheard, but since he's forgotten to bring slippers we buy him a pair of leather slip-ons, a useful souvenir of Ukraine. I add two small wooden dishes made from beech wood, the lady in the shop tells me, Hutsul work from the Carpathians; I recall Masha in Lutsk who sold me her own embroidery. Perhaps one day we'll go to the Carpathians . . . perhaps . . .

For now, we explore Zhitomir.

We chat to a student who is going off to a Polish class. He tells us there's still a sizeable Polish community in Zhitomir and as proof of that we come upon a brand new Roman Catholic church, big and grandiose like the Russian one they were building in Berezhany. A life-size statue of Pope John Paul II, whose mother was Ukrainian, blesses the congregation. We don't go inside but instead visit a museum housed in a former palace. The elderly curator nobbles Stuart. I drift away but hear from snatches of conversation that this man is voicing negative stuff about the present state of things in the new independent Ukraine. It's clear that life is hard for many people. We walk towards the bus station – I should say hobble, because Stuart's knee has finally given up, his operation is fixed for the end of the month. Stuart wants to check on the bus timetable for our eventual return to Kyiv. A woman sits on the pavement. She's selling old shoes and has spread them out singly on a large piece of polythene, obviously aware that they might 'walk' if she put them in pairs. Amongst this worn footwear is a small sandal. It was once clear plastic, now it's dirty and torn and shaped to the contours of its previous owner's foot. In their expensively constructed enclosure with their diet of fruit, regular veterinary check-ups, cruelly treated though they had been, our bears are privileged creatures compared to this shabby woman and to whichever child will force her foot into this poor little shoe.

As we too are fortunate, for we can afford to stay here and enjoy meals in the cafes and restaurants of the town, one of which informs us that the French writer Balzac was here – we had come across his name in Hotel George in Lviv. It seems he was in pursuit of a much younger (of course!) aristocratic lady.

We can also easily afford a visit to the hairdresser and a pedicure. I recall a wonderful hairdo I once had in Kyiv and so I tell Stuart he should get his hair cut here, not that he has much hair, but there's always his beard as well. While that's happening, a pedicurist in a corner of the salon is only too happy to do my feet. To my dismay she only has an emery board to smooth hard dry skin. She tells me how hard life is with young adult children who are obviously causing lots of bother. However, she benefits, because the banknote I pull out of my wallet is probably more than she earns all week. It was larger than I had intended, but still the whole procedure has cost less than a pedicure at home. She's totally delighted, not to say overwhelmed, so it's a win-win situation. "High heaven rejects the lore of nicely calculated less and more," says Wordsworth, though I always feel that he was probably a bit of a meanie himself.

Light of foot (and of purse), I join Stuart on a wander through the town. Communism engulfed Eastern Europe like a tsunami, and when it withdrew it left detritus, rubbish of all kinds, a broken society. A hundred years, give or take a decade, of a totalitarian regime leaves its mark, but the future lies with the young and we happen upon an open-air concert. A girl with flowers in her hair and an embroidered skirt which rides up above slender knees sings and accompanies herself on the folk instrument, the bandura. Electronics added to the sound system give traditional melodies a modern slant; the crowd who gathers hugely enjoys the concert. It's modern, yet traditional, it's 'ours'.

Spring is coming to Zhitomir. Early blossom brightens trees in back yards. Small blue flowers push through the grass and when the sun shines, it's gratifyingly warm.

We catch a crowded bus out to the Bear Centre. Young guys jump up to offer Stuart a seat – it goes without saying that they do the same for me. With his pending operation, he's using a walking stick – and there's a story about that stick.

He bought it in a pharmacy on a previous visit to Kyiv. It's just a bog standard stick, no inner spring or any way of changing its height. But what a bargain! It had cost the equivalent of £2.50. So he showed it proudly to friends he was visiting in the historic town of Chernihiv, about ninety miles north of Kyiv. They were horrified. Wha-at!!!! You spent all that money on a walking stick!

These eighty year olds, Petya and Raya live only off food they grow themselves in an allotment out of town. They can't afford the taxi buses like minicabs that we usually use. They have to wait for the local bus, ancient and decrepit and so unreliable that they often have to walk. Petya was born in Uman, the town now much visited by Orthodox Jews. His wife, Raya grew up in the USSR outside Chelyabinsk, beyond the Urals. Ukrainian? Russian? No, they were Soviet citizens until Ukraine became independent and, more importantly to them, members of the much persecuted unregistered Baptist congregation. In fact Raya's younger sister, Aida is the reason why we have both been focussed on Russia for most our lives. Stuart met Aida way back in summer 1961, just a few months before he met me, they were both twenty-one.

He was on a British Council funded language course in what was then Leningrad. He looked for a non-Orthodox church. The women in the travel bureau created a fuss. "What's a young man like you doing, going to church? Church is for old grannies."

A girl came up to him after the service. "Help me, I want to believe," she said.

"Why don't you speak to the pastor?" he asked. His Russian was only minimal at that point and he was flummoxed when she said. "I don't trust the pastor, and I trust the elders even less."

Later he realised that for any church, synagogue or temple to stay open it had to be registered and the state planted their own functionaries in the leadership.

Aida found faith – and persecution. During a bleak post-graduate year in Leningrad 1963-64 when our letters took three weeks and were read by two different censors, Stuart sent me covert news about 'our friend'. If he could catch a foreigner, usually an American, going 'out' to Helsinki or Stockholm, he wrote more openly. Those letters burnt a figurative hole in my bag as I travelled across Glasgow. I quote from memory after all these years:

> A. came to my hostel today. This was unwise as visits to a foreigner are noted. She brought cuttings from the official press. A photo of children with their hands clasped in prayer and the caption, 'Obscurantists! These children have now been taken from their parents who taught them to do such vile things.'

This was in the days of particularly harsh repression launched by the Soviet leader Nikita Krushchev against all forms of belief. There's clearly nothing new in a Russian president authorising the kidnapping of children.

Another letter told me that Aida had broken all the rules and had headed to Ukraine to stay with her sister. You were not allowed to travel more than thirty miles beyond the place where you were registered and the police were waiting for her when she tried to get back. She outwitted them, but the point is, that it was because she'd broken the thirty mile limit and not because she'd crossed any borders. Soviet Ukraine had been so completely swallowed up by Soviet Russia that it didn't seem like a different country.

Aida had wanted to go to Ukraine because, as she put it, she found faith there burning like a forest fire and she wanted to be part of it – though she suffered for it, first one year and then three years in prison, forced to do menial jobs and to register with the police every year until 1989.

All that came from a walking stick!

Stuart also told me that in the historic part of Chernihiv he had noticed a plaque put up in 1954 which commemorated the 300 years since the Ukrainian hero Bohdan Khmelnytsky's alliance with the Russian Tsar 1654 when Ukraine entered into 'an eternal union' with Russia. To celebrate this union in 1954 Krushchev transferred Crimea to Ukraine, a political as well as symbolic gesture which has enormous consequences today when Putin has illegally taken it and claims that it still belongs to Russia. I should add it's a straight road from Kyiv to Chernihiv and we were appalled when Russian tanks rolled along it in March 2022 and bombarded the historic town.

Back to the bears. We buy a big plastic tub of honey for them and Sasha is touched and delighted. He's a bit preoccupied today because a television crew is filming the Nadiya Centre and the bears – and oh dear, they want to film us too. Stuart pushes me forward. "Tell them about Wojtek the bear who fought in the war." "No, you do it, your Russian is so good . . ." "No, you wrote the book, you do it."

So here I am in the April sunshine with bears all about me as I tell an unseen audience the story of the brown bear who fought in the Second World War and is now honoured with a statue in Scotland's capital city.

Next morning at breakfast we appear on the large television screen in the hotel dining room and I hear myself express my appreciation of the bear rescue centre and retell the story of Wojtek in Russian.

We're sorry to leave Ukraine but we've got two dates ahead. Stuart's knee operation and before that, we have been invited to appear on a chat show on Polish television. What bad timing! We could have travelled by train to Warsaw. Instead, we'd already booked flights from Kyiv to Edinburgh.

At the airport the official who checks our passports looks at us in surprise. "I recognise you." she says. "Didn't I see you on morning TV talking about bears?" We have a good laugh and chat.

This television chat show is also bad timing because now we have to switch from Russian to Polish in front of the cameras and a few thousand – or however many – viewers.

On the way home we travel by train from Newcastle. The conductor who checks our tickets looks at us in surprise. "My mother saw two Scottish people on Polish television talking about bears. Was it you? I must tell Mum that I've met you!" He takes a selfie with us to send to his mother.

Now we're back in Scotland. Will we ever return to Ukraine? We've 'done' the archives, we've visited historic towns and castles, we've seen the bears. Of course we must go back because Ukraine is beautiful and there are still so many places to visit, especially the Carpathians.

Chapter 5

The Carpathians

Kolomyia and the Carpathians

Our next visit to Ukraine is to Kolomyia a small town with a good network of buses to take visitors into the Carpathians. At least that's what one of the guide books says. We fly to Warsaw and stay with friends, then take a flight to Lviv. I feel that there is something very special about this particular flight. For a start we're leaving from a 'proper' airport, not the barracks that Ryanair uses miles out of the city. And to fly from here to Lviv feels somehow wholly European and yet also different, slightly off the beaten track and very precious. This is partly because Lviv had been so very closed off, partly too because so many people so deeply regretted the loss of this city and also because there's an aura about Lviv that makes you feel that you need your best clothes, just the same as people in Edinburgh in the days of long lost elegance felt about the late lamented Jenner's. You couldn't possibly shop there without your hat, gloves and pearl necklace.

The people on our flight obviously don't wear hats, gloves or pearl necklaces and I can't help recalling a KLM flight from Amsterdam to Kyiv when the rather small aeroplane filled up with rather large passengers. I'm not thinking about obesity, oh no. Ukrainians enjoy hearty meals, and a favourite dish is *salo*, which we would know as dripping, rich fat from a joint of meat, with onions and garlic. It's highly calorific, much needed to keep out the cold if you're fishing in ice-pools in winter. People work hard. Women still wash clothes without machines and dig in their allotments. Men turn skilful hands to all manner of DIY jobs at home or for friends.

It took time to settle passengers and copious hand luggage in this plane and take off was a delayed. Stuart and I were in the second last row. The plane had a bit of a struggle to become airborne, and about twenty minutes later we felt a worrying jolt, as if something had dropped off the bottom of the plane, but no, it was okay and we continued our flight. However, forty-five minutes into the flight the plane did turn back. We were told that another plane was being made ready for us, we must wait on the tarmac outside the departure lounge. No smoking was allowed. Naturally all the smokers lit up at once. A long time afterwards we boarded a much bigger plane, passengers, goods and gear were comfortably bestowed and we touched down safely in Kyiv at 3.30 am.

Luckily there are no such issues on our present flight except that Stuart's infallible satnav doesn't seem to function in Lviv and we trail our cases around as we look for somewhere to eat. It's very warm, you could even say hot, the end of another *babie leto*, Indian summer so I'm hoping for good weather in Kolomyia. We eat in a busy self-service café and trudge off again. No sight-seeing today and indeed once we're on the busy train there are no views at all. Our seats are jammed up against an end wall with no windows. It's a four hour journey, very cramped and uncomfortable and pitch dark when we arrive at 10 pm. The taxi driver has no idea where our hotel might be. He parks near an unlit building in an empty square and drives off. This is worrying. There are steps to be climbed up to an inhospitably closed door. It opens eventually, yes, this is the right place. We've booked bed and breakfast. Bed is okay, but no breakfast, the restaurant doesn't open in the mornings. "There's a café across the square," the man says, gives us keys and we settle in.

The café only does coffee and croissants, very nice at mid-day but we'd hoped for something a bit more substantial for breakfast. Still, the sun is shining, so what are we waiting for? The Hutsul museum, of course, to find out all about these mountain people and their culture. The curator shows us the huge Alpine horn which, when blown, uttered a deep mooing sound that carried across the hillsides. We examine wooden utensils, see what a typical cottage was like, look at intricate, colourful embroidery and watch a video of a Hutsul wedding, which could last for days.

CAROLS IN OLD VILLAGE TRANSCARPATHIA [*PHOTO BY PELLINNI*]

Kolomyia is quiet and clean, but war and the shifting powers that constantly took possession of Ukraine certainly didn't pass the tranquil town by. It was very much a border town, so close to Romania, that it had many changes of government and hadn't been spared the bloodletting in the Second World War or the Kremlin's iron first. We cross a large square which reminds us of the one we saw in Berezhany, here too we imagine that we can hear the strains of the Radetsky march and see the troops out in full splendour – as they certainly were when the city fathers garlanded the town with flowers in 1912. This was to welcome the Hapsburg Emperor's grandson, the Archduke Charles and his wife Zita just two years before the fatal shots in Sarajevo that killed Charles' father and mother and plunged Europe into war.

You can't miss Kolomyia's most colourful building. Called *Pysanka* after the art of egg painting it's shaped like a huge painted egg. If I were here with my sister we would have visited the museum and spent ages examining the different patterns of all the many elaborately painted eggs – and spent ages in the museum shop as well. Instead I drag my unwilling husband through the covered market where, amidst pots and pans, cleaning products, socks, slippers, underwear of all shapes and sizes, in short, all the essentials of daily life, I at last find the thing I've been looking for on our travels, a traditional fleecy waistcoat. I take it back to the hotel in triumph.

Easter eggs [*photo by AnSyvan*]

Did I mention the Radetsky March? No need to use our imagination today. A brass band strikes up under our hotel window. The musicians are all male and all wear the inevitable embroidered shirts. They play traditional tunes with lots of enthusiasm, then take themselves off somewhere and we too go off to look around some more.

As we cross the square outside our hotel, I notice two women in wheelchairs and suddenly realise I haven't seen any wheelchairs, invalid buggies or even any children or adults with physical difficulties on our explorations. I know that children are born with alcohol syndrome and all manner of other syndromes because of drink and drugs, but we don't see them out and about or on buses or trains.

These two women are giving out booklets, helped by two other women who might be American. They're Jehovah's Witnesses, it feels as if the wheelchair users in this prominent place is part of a publicity statement.

We browse through a second hand shop with books and folk art, I buy straw stars and angels for the Christmas tree. Then, still following Hutsuls, we discover a tourist office. Solomia is in charge. She and her husband Denys will give us a ride into the Carpathians tomorrow. Their thirty year old car struggles gallantly along almost empty roads and we soon get views of the hills. We stop at a viewing point. Denys tells us that people do paragliding from here, it's a great lift-off place.

We climb higher. The River Prut tumbles below in rushing waterfalls. People scramble across wet rocks dangerously close to the churning water. The tourist centre and main town of the region is called Yaremche. It reminds us of Zakopane in the Polish Tatra Mountains, we both agree that if we were ever to have a holiday in the Carpathians we'd start from here.

There are eating places and souvenir stalls which sell Hutsul carvings, embroidery, leather and sheepskins. I should have liked to have lingered but prices which seem cheap to us are far from cheap for our hosts.

We park the car and walk through the woods, the trees are mainly conifers. We find stout sticks to help us on the uphill path. Grannies with little kids are on the trail too and manage fine unaided. Denys keeps disappearing and then re-appearing with a huge grin and even bigger objects –mushrooms the like of which I'd never seen. He names each one. He's an expert and mushroom gathering is a passion.

Our guides take us along a marked trail. A poster in Ukrainian and English tells us that, "Starting on the trail you enter the living museum of nature which is the unique source of natural values and needs to be loved and protected."

Yes, indeed! A map indicates various walks of various lengths. The trail is called after a folk hero, Oleksa Dovbush. He's shown on horseback in Hutsul dress. He's the Ukrainian Robin Hood, an eighteenth century outlaw who robbed the rich and gave money and goods to the poor.

He hid out in the hills with his gang of outlaws and terrorised and plundered the local landowners, some of whom, including the Pototsky clan, tried to capture him but failed. His fame spread throughout the mountains and into Podillya and West Ukraine. He's the subject of folk songs and legends. Ruthless and cruel, he could also show kindness. One story says he was about to raid the manor house of the Karpiński family but when he saw the lady of the house nursing her new born child, he did her no harm and gave her three gold coins for herself and her baby.

I was glad to hear this because this baby grew up to become the author and composer of one of Poland's most loved Christmas carols, *Bóg się rodzi* . . . God is born.

The Hutsul hero Dovbush was eventually killed by a fellow Hutsul, a jealous husband, whose wife had become the lover of the great adventurer.

Following our walk we enjoy a late lunch in a wooden chalet-style restaurant with views of the hills. And there too I enjoy a local speciality: tea brewed from the herbs of the Carpathians.

Solomia gives me a gift, a set of postcards which depict the work of her father, a graphic artist and wood carver. Most of the selection has Christian themes and she stresses how dangerous that was for him in the Soviet area – he could never put such work on display.

Much later I see posts on Facebook which reveal that Solomia actively promotes her town and also offers refuge to people from war torn areas of Ukraine.

I discover that we're not the only British visitors to have come to Kolomyia and explore Hutsul culture. The railway at the end of the nineteenth century brought the 'English', including Scots visitors. Gents in bowler hats, plus fours and heavy tweeds mingled with Hutsul mountaineers in Highland dress, the women wrapped in colourful shawls, as well as with Jewish business men and traders, also typically dressed. One of the most striking of these exotic visitors was a young woman who claimed Scottish descent though she had been born in Liverpool. Ménie Muriel Dowie was still in her early twenties when she strode forth in tartan with a Tam o' Shanter bunnet and a long cigarette holder. A woman smoking in the street scandalised the genteel Polish community. They would have been more appalled if they had seen her head off alone to remote Hutsul villages in the mountains. Her Hutsul ponies were too small for the saddles she had brought from home. She often walked to let the horses rest. She spoke German to the villagers, having lived for some time in Stuttgart, but learnt some Polish and what she called Ruthenian phrases. She acted like a superior being, was utterly and invariably nasty about Jews whom she met on her travels, she committed unknowingly all sorts of social and cultural faux pas, but she was no wimp. She ate all the food she was given. Wild swimming was no novelty: she bathed in river water with dangerous depths and currents. She would climb the hills and walk all day in her tweed knickerbockers with only berries for sustenance, sleep rough and emerge covered with flea bites which she soothed by rubbing snow over her arms and face. On one occasion a servant girl cut her finger off while she was chopping meat. The onlookers broke into an outcry of horror. Ménie tore up a pinafore, made a tourniquet and pulled cobwebs from the rafters to staunch the wound. The girl lost her finger but not her life and the chain smoking young foreign woman was regarded with special awe and gratitude in that village.

Our enjoyable walk on the Dovbush Trail paled beside Miss Dowie's exploits. She was a suffragette, feminist ahead of her time, a free-thinking woman whose only son was tragically killed in an aircraft accident in the Second World War. Following her adventures in the Carpathians, Ménie wrote a best-selling book about her travels and was invited to give talks and lectures.

The end of our time in Kolomyia coincides with water being cut off in the town and with the end of the warm weather. Icy rain lashes us as we wait on the platform for a train back to Lviv and when we get to the station the queues at the ticket office for Poland are endless, so many, many people leave Ukraine to work in Poland or Germany. The bus we catch in Lviv is busy too. We're the only tourists. Everybody travels out of necessity to make money.

We cruise through the countryside, sometimes stopping to give way to cows and their calves. There are long queues at the border. Brexit hasn't happened yet and it's only too clear that these sort of delays will lie ahead for British travellers if we leave the EU.

It's dark when we reach Kraków. We're the only people who get off here. And so we leave Ukraine.

Is it goodbye for ever? Yes, it is. A year later I was diagnosed with myeloma, an incurable bone marrow cancer and in 2021 Stuart suffered two strokes and has no movement in his right arm or leg. And so I travel with you by sharing these memories and hope that when the war is over – and let that be soon – you will explore the historic cities, the great waterways, lakes and mountains of Ukraine.

Chapter 6

Poems

Elegy: Small Jewish Towns

Antoni Słonimski (1895-1976), translated Stuart and Jenny Robertson

No more, no more *shtetlen** in Poland,
whether in Hrubieszów, Karczew, Brody or Falenica
you'd be hard put to find lit candles in their windows,
or catch the strains of song in wooden synagogues.

The last vestiges of Jewish life have gone;
blood covered over with sand,   all traces swept away,
walls whitened with fresh coats of lime
as if some plague had passed, or a feast is welcomed in.
Here the moon shines solitary, alien, chill, and pale.
Out of town, on the highway, where night is ablaze,
my Jewish kinsfolk, *makars aa,* will not find
Chagall's two golden moons.

Those moons illumine another planet now,
they fled, frightened by the sombre silence.
The *shtetlen* are no more where the cobbler was a poet,
the watchmaker a philosopher, barber a troubadour.

The *shtetlen* are no more where Bible chants
swirled on the wind with Polish song and Slav lament,
where Jewish grandfathers, secluded in a cherry orchard,
wept for the holy walls of Jerusalem.

Those *shtetlen* are no more, vanished like a shadow,
and this shadow will intrude between our words
until the advent of brotherhood, unity renewed:
two nations nourished by centuries of suffering.

* Plural of shtetl, Yiddish for a small town where most habitants are Jewish

The following poems are © Jenny Robertson . . .

Children

Do you see those sunlit children,
Moshele, Shosha, Heim
barefoot in summer meadows –
camomile, cornflower, thyme.
Such sun-warmed, love-gathered posies
for cottage-loaved, apple-cheeked Mam!

Do you see their bare feet run
between barbed wire, dogs and guns?
Safe now – oh, frail flowers!
Jankiel and that little one
whose pinafore pink as roses
flutters in summer sun.

They dance, those sunlit children,
– shoes removed and neatly laced.
Carefree, bright as daisies –
Ruta, Estera, Staś.
No glimpse yet of their faces.
Mother's cheeks are pale as ash.

They will never grow old, those children,
Avrom, Izaak, Imest . . .
A skylark sings: *Remember*!
A stork wings to her nest.

Wraith-like against sun's last ember
children fade in twilit mist.

Lutsk: no glitz, no bill

Western business promotes
salts and salves, soft ambience. You float
in brine, light-limbed like astronauts, then sweat
in steam. Next, caked in wholesome dirt,
relax, recline. The mud, the heat will treat
tension, stress, bring ease, respite
to ravelled nerves, make whole
the unseen, secret workings of the soul.

Outside, steep paths lead to the swell
and eddy of the river. Bathers all
year strip and dip, despite the chill
of water, earth and air. Emerge tranquil.

This remedy is free. No glitz, no bill.

Yaslovets

Silence. Brown hens scratch
in the dusty path outside
a white-walled church,
a former Armenian shrine.

Armenian?
So, there were once furred merchants here, ornate homes,
gems clustered like pomegranates, while ritual lambs
were sacrificed each Easter in this quiet place?

The Polish presence is revealed
by roofless walls and broken brick
where hussars sported splendid swords,
princes plotted, rosaries clicked
and poets composed epic words.

Jewish memories drift, sunlit.
Here Baal Shem Tov's deep wisdom smiled,
a goodly blessing gone! And gone
all else. O, rich dark earth, what music
has died for ever beneath the heedless ground?

Now there is only sunlight on long grass
and stories lost for ever, speech grown strange
in Yaslovets, Podillya, West Ukraine.

Zhitomir, second-hand sweat

Where ripening rye, sign
of sufficiency, is aligned
with peace, Zhitomir,
'an uneventful place'
a guidebook opines,
though armies marched
and ravaged here.

Vikings rolled dragon prows over inland seas,
Settling, turned charts to charters,
donned ducal crowns, bowed reluctant knees
to khan and knout.

Shifting tides of war and merchandise
smelted language for each ruler's speech.
The most recent ruthless host
has crushed this city in a fraternal fist.

And so we trace the past
among forgotten tombs with lost
names inscribed on fractured stones.

The present is spelt out in battered shoes
lined for sale singly in the street,
A child will cram her growing feet
into shoes creased to a stranger's fit.

No guide books describe second hand sweat:
this story no tourist reads in Zhitomir.

High fashion

The catwalk hits the small town street.
Money goes to women's feet.

Boots knee high, heels
thin and sharp as nails
wobble across cobbles, cut
paved setts, ill-set.

Worn with shortest skirts,
with briefest shorts, culottes –
Prince Charming on the strut.

each pair's a work of art!
Laced, be-ribboned, brazen, bright,
tipped toe and heel, metallic, tight.

Blazoning high fashion, such extravagance
throws sobriety down the drain.
Such power dressing must be caught
on camera in today's Ukraine.

West Ukraine before Putin's war

The Kyiv express trundles towards a country town
so slowly you can count the trees or orchestrate
the symphony sunlight plays on branch and bough,
grace-notes of amber, russet, brown.

    Birches wear a radiant crown.

So beautiful this land, so little known:
lost lyric rich in memory; lush earth sown
with crumbled castles, abandoned graves. Ukraine,
land that time forgot, though war and tyranny have not.

    Apples bend
the boughs of village trees.
Vines entwine eaves of weathered thatch,
while hens, ignorant of cages, peck and scratch.

Sunflowers lift heavy heads towards the light.
Cornflowers, poppies, marguerites
embroider fields ripe with wheat
where Moshe, Shosha once took trembling cover.

    Oh, plover, plaintive in long grass,
    tell me when the children pass.

    Oh, hawks that spy
    scurrying things with unblinking eye,
    tell me where those small ones lie.

    A shower of leaves – sheerest lace
    shrouds an unmarked burial place.

No synagogue now, no Hebrew school.
You buy train tickets in the shul.
The Armenian temple is a swimming pool;
Strzeletski's villa is a plush motel.

Our Lady of Mercy's walls are bare:
no Polish rosaries are murmured there –
but autumn's bounty fills the market square.

Twilight signals the Kyiv express,
a long night journey in reverse.
        Crowds cross the rails.

Young women, arm-in arm, on highest heels,
old women drag home-grown goods for sale.
Men in black caps, roll-ups tossed away,
heave mighty bundles city-wards to trade,
travel on hardest seats. The old, betrayed
by empty promises, journey to survive,
to keep drug-addicted children's bairns alive,
        offer purple asters, sweetest plums,
        woven napkins, honey-combs.
Shapeless as their bundles, doze and snore.

Newspapers for tablecloths are spread
as neighbours sprinkle salt on hard-won bread.

The silent ones

Seated in a sunlit corner

–   wasp time, plum time,
beyond the hum of traffic,
I sense a presence,
an alter-ego, guessed at,

yet not my own, no, not my own.

It is the long slow walk of folk unknown
through lands and borders beset
with bombs. So this
is why I am what I am. I write
the loss and cost of those,
the silent ones, without name or home.

Chapter 7

Historical Notes

St Andrew and Scottish connections:

The great Declaration of Arbroath of 1320) reminds the Pope that:

> even though they (the Scots) lived at the furthermost ends of the Earth, the King of kings and the Lord of lords, Jesus Christ after His Passion and His Resurrection, called them *nearly the first* to his most Holy Faith. Nor did He want to confirm them in the said Faith by anyone but *the first to be an Apostle* . . . the brother of the Blessed Peter, gentle Saint Andrew . . .
>
> [*The Declaration of Arbroath*, my italics]

This pointed reminder that, according to John's gospel, Andrew met Jesus before Peter (John 1: 40-42) makes the Scots upsides with the Pope. It leads to the great declaration for freedom:

> As long as but a hundred of us remain alive, never will we on any conditions be brought under English rule. It is in truth not for glory, nor riches, nor honours, that we are fighting, but for freedom - for that alone, which no honest man gives up but with life itself (ibid).

These proud words resonate today in the daily life – and death – of every Ukrainian as the nation suffers bombardment and destruction in the current illegal war.

Who's Who

Rabbi Nahman (1772 – 1810) a Hassid master, follower of Baal Shem Tov.

Baal Shem Tov (1698 – 1760) the Master of the Good Name, founded the Hasidic movement which spread widely through Podillya and Volyn.

Mikhail Bulgakov (1894 – 1940), Russian writer, educated in Kyiv where he wrote *The White Guard* and *The Turbins*. His novel, *The Master and Marguerita* was published only after his death.

Wannsee conference, 20th January 1942, set the seal on the deportation to Poland and murder of every single Jewish child, woman and man in Europe.

Henryk Sienkiewicz (1846 – 1916) Nobel Prize winner, best known beyond Poland for the novel *Quo Vadis* and in Poland for his *Trilogy*, *With Fire and Sword*, *Deluge* and *Sir Wołodyjowkski* set in embattled Poland in the 17th century. The recent film by Jerzy Hoffman, 1999 is well worth watching.

Stanisław August Poniatowski (1732 – 1798), the last king of Poland. The country was partitioned after his forced abdication.

Bohdan Khmelnytskiy (1595 – 1657) Cossack leader who tried to win independence but at the cost of a Treaty in 1654 which put Ukraine under the control of the Russian Tsar.

The Marshal and President of Poland, **Józef Piłsudski** (1867 – 1935), an unforgettable figure, Piłsudski wanted to form a federation of Poland, Ukraine and Lithuania to act as a buffer state against the Bolsheviks.

Leonid Brezhnev (1906 – 1982) Born in Ukraine, but claiming Russian ethnicity, he rose to be General Secretary of the Communist Party of the USSR.

Honoré Balzac (1799 – 1850) French novelist who comes into our story because a love affair which brought him to Zhitomir and Lviv.

Adam Mickiewicz (1798 – 1855) A Romantic poet and Poland's national bard. Born in what is now Belarus and educated in Vilnius, he never actually lived within the boundaries of today's Poland. A recent film by Andrzej Wajda was based on the much-loved epic poem.

Stalin's Revenge: The playwright is Aleksander Fredro, 1793, died in Lviv in 1876.

In the confused aftermath of the First World War, Ukraine and Poland sought independence. In 1920, Polish forces stormed Kyiv and claimed Galicia,

Volyhnia and Podole, lands that had historically belonged to Poland. The Communist leader Lenin in Moscow believed that war-torn Europe was ready for revolution and that Poland would never resist his armies. 'Over the corpse of White Poland lies the road to World Conflagration. On our bayonets we will bring happiness and peace to the toiling masses of mankind.' the quote comes from Adam Zamoyski, *Warsaw 1920, Lenin's failed conquest of Europe*, Harper Press 2008 p.53)

The accounts of Polish resettlement are found variously, including in *moje wojenne dzieciństwo*, my wartime childhood, a series of memoirs, published by a private foundation, Warsaw.

UPA (the Ukrainian Insurgent Army) and **UON** (the Organisation of Ukrainian Nationalists), both groups supported the idea of independence through violence and carried out brutal ethnic cleansing against Poles and Jews in Volyn and East Galicia in 1943-44. Active until 1949, although officially disbanded, the groups were viewed as terrorists by the Soviets, arrested, tortured, killed. Veterans have been rehabilitated in today's Ukraine and their greeting, *Slava Ukraini*, Glory to Ukraine, is now widely used.

The writer who praised Kremenets (Krzemieniec) as the most beautiful town in Poland was **Ksawery Pruszyński** (1907 – 1950) in *Podróż po Polsce*, Czytelnik, Warszaw 2000 p, 136). Born in Volyn, Pruszyński, a journalist, poet and diplomat, served in the Polish Army in Scotland and died in Germany in what may not have been an accident.

Stepan Bandera (1909 – 1959) Regarded by many as a hero and true patriot, by others as a fascist and murderer, Bandera was committed to nationalism and independence for Ukraine, he become leader of the Organisation of Ukrainian Nationalists. Imprisoned in Poland, following an assassination of a political leader, he was later in concentration camp in Germany when his followers in the Organisation of Ukrainian Nationalists carried out brutal murders of the Polish population, so it's not clear how much Bandera himself knew about the atrocious killings. He was assassinated in Germany by a KGB agent.

Alexander Naismyth, or Nasmyth (1758 – 1840) Scottish landscape poet.

Taras Shevchenko (1814 – 1861) Ukraine's national poet, Shevchenko was born into a serf family and knew poverty and harsh treatment. He managed to become literate and in spite of severe repression, developed as a talented artist. Eventually the artist circle in St Petersburg put one of his paintings up for lottery and with its proceeds set him free. Shevchenko became known as *Kobzar*, the ballad singer and through his work the Ukrainian language and its poetry reached high literary levels. Few poets and artists can have laboured under such difficulties and suffered such harsh treatment, the Soviets even destroyed the cross above his grave, but Taras Shevchenko has found much deserved fame and high renown in his native Ukraine.

Tadeusz Czacki (1765 – 1813), a great and genial figure, Czacki worked tirelessly on behalf of education and true enlightenment. He funded and founded the Lyceum in today's Kremenets, worked tirelessly for Jewish emancipation and wrote works which explored Jewish history and persecution. He died in Dubno where we saw a plaque to commemorate him.

Canon Hugo Kołłątaj (1750 – 1812), a priest, poet, politician, holder of several doctorates, and not unfamiliar with the inside of several prisons, Kołłątaj, along with Czacki was part of the Commission for National Education.

Juliusz Słowacki (1809 – 1849) Born and brought up in Kremenets, also in Vilnius. Słowacki chose exile and died almost alone and unhonoured in Paris, though later acknowledged as one of the great bards of Poland. His body was taken to Poland in 1927 and was buried in the crypt of Wawel Cathedral in Kraków among the kings of Poland, because, said Marshall Piłsudski, he is equal to them all.

Queen Bona (1494 – 1557) became wife of the Polish king Zygmunt. She was titled Queen of Poland, Grand Duchess of Lithuania, Rus and Prus and was a powerful, but also cruel figure.

Pochayiv Lavra, a great monastic complex with two Cathedrals and a monastery, the Lavra has stood firm under attack both during war and virulent atheism. It's a major centre of pilgrimage in the town of Pochayiv outside Kremenets.

Rainer Maria Rilke (1875 – 1926) Austrian lyric poet and writer.

Lesya Ukrainka (Larysa Kosach) 1871-1913) poet, writer and translator who chose to write in Ukrainian and used the pseudonym by which she is now widely known.

Edward Rydz-Śmigły (1886 – 1941) Marshal of Poland and commander of the Armed Forces, blamed not entirely fairly for the Polish defeat in 1939.

Cossacks – adventurers, seekers of freedom, runaway serfs and outlaws, eventually banded together to become a powerful fighting force used by the Polish kings who controlled what is now West Ukraine and eventually the Russian Tsars. There are Cossack groups in southern Russia as well as in Ukraine.

Samuel Agnon (1888 – 1970) Nobel Prize winner, Agnon was born in Buchach and lived eventually in Israel. His literary works in Hebrew are acknowledged masterpieces.

Emanuel Ringelblum (1900 – 1944) Another son of Buchach, Ringelblum is best known for his work in the Warsaw ghetto where he and other incarcerated inmates created an important archive which detailed events of the annihilation of Jewish life in Poland, Ukraine and Lithuania as it happened. They worked in conditions of hunger and terror until, knowing that they, along with the whole community were doomed, they hid the documents in three milk churns and two large tin boxes which they buried in the ghetto. Ringelblum, his wife and son along with thirteen others were hidden by a Polish family. They were betrayed and executed, along with their would-be rescuers. Before his death, incarcerated with his son in the infamous Pawiak prison, Ringelblum was tortured for three days. Friends in the Jewish underground tried to rescue him, but couldn't save his wife or son. Ringelblum refused. His last recorded words were '*Voz iz er shuldik, der kleyner? Tsulib em veytigt mir shtark dos harts.*' What is he guilty of, the little one? My heart breaks because of him.'

Simon Wiesenthal (1908 – 2005) Also born in Buchach, Wiesenthal dedicated his life to bringing Nazi war criminals to justice.

Jan III Sobieski (1629 – 1696) King of Poland, famous for defeating the Ottoman forces at Vienna in 1683, Charles Edward Stuart was descended from that family.

Yasloviets, town in Ukraine, near Buchach, it features in *Emancypantki*, a novel by one of Poland's greatest nineteenth century writers and gave its name to a famous Polish regiment.

The writer is **Maria Janion** (1926 – 2020), in a collection of essays called 'To Europe yes, together with our dead.'

Nikita Khrushchev (1894 – 1971) General Secretary of the Communist Party, gave Crimea to Soviet Ukraine in 1954.

Books

I used two Polish guide books, *Wołyń, Podole*, Gregorz Rąkowski, Pruszków 2005, 2006 and Andrew Evans, Ukraine, The Bradt Travel Guide *www.bradtguides.com*.

For the history:

Samuel D. Kassow, *Who will write our history?* Penguin, London 2007
Serhii Plokhy, *The Gates of Europe, a history of Ukraine*, Penguin, London 2016
Ryszard Przybylski, *Krzemieniec*, Sic! Warsaw 2003
Jenny Robertson, *Ghetto*, Lion 1989
                 Don't go to Uncle's Wedding, Azure/SPCK 2000

Travel and memoir:

Isaac Babel, *Red Cavalry and other stories*, Penguin, London 1994
Sister Wendy Beckett, *Encounters with God*, Continuum, London 2009
Andrew Bonar & R.M. McCheyne, *Mission of Discovery*, reissued Christian
    Focus, Fearn
Maria Chamberlain, *Never tell anyone you're Jewish*, Vallentine Mitchell, London 2022
Ménie Muriel Dowie, *A girl in the Carpathians*, reissued Cassell Publishing
Marek Feldman, *From Warsaw through Łuck, Siberia . . .* Feldman lulu, 2009
Jason Francisco, *An Unfinished Memory*, Centre of Urban History, Kraków 2014
Rabbi Nachman, *Opowieści*, sel. & ed. Henryk Hałkowski, Mercury, Warsaw 1999
Anna Pruszyńska, *Między Bohem a Słuczą*, Ossolineum, Wrocław, 1999
Ksawery Pruszyński, *Podróż po Polsce*, Czytelnik, Warsaw, 2000
Philippe Sands, *East West Street*, Weidenfeld and Nicolson, London 2016
Philippe Sands, *The Ratline*, Weidenfeld and Nicolson, London 2020
Eva Stachniak, *Garden of Venus*, Harper Collins, London 2005
Timothy Snyder, *The Red Prince*, The Bodley Head, London 2008,
Joseph Tarnowski, *Walking with Shadows*, Glen Murray Publishing, 2009
Roman Vishniac *Vanished World* Penguin, London 1986
Józef Wittlin, Philippe Sands, *City of Lions*, Pushkin Press, London 2016
Józef Wittlin, *The Salt of the Earth*, translated Patrick John Corness, foreword
    by Philippe Sands, Pushkin Press, London 2018